SPEAKING TO A GROUP

Mastering the SKILL
of public speaking

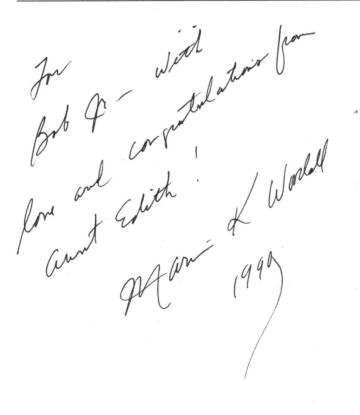

For
Bob J— with
love and congratulations from
aunt Edith !
Marie K Woodall
(199?)

Also by Marian K. Woodall

Thinking On Your Feet — softcover
Thinking On Your Feet — audio cassette

SPEAKING TO A GROUP

Mastering the SKILL
of public speaking

MARIAN K. WOODALL

PBC
PROFESSIONAL BUSINESS COMMUNICATIONS

Lake Oswego, Oregon 97035

SPEAKING TO A GROUP

Printed in the United States of America

Current printing (last digit):
10 9 8 7 6 5 4 3 2 1

Library of Congress Cataloging-in-Publication Data

Woodall, Marian K., 1941–
    Speaking to a group : mastering the skill of public speaking / Marian K. Woodall.
        p.   cm.
      ISBN 0-941159-02-7 : $15.95
      1. Public speaking.   I. Title.
PN4121.W586   1989   89-27258
808.5′1 – dc20   CIP

Published and Distributed by
PROFESSIONAL BUSINESS COMMUNICATIONS
11830 S.W. Kerr Parkway, Suite 350
Lake Oswego, Oregon 97035

DEDICATION

To Dr. William B. Hunter, Jr.,
who taught me—by both example and advice—
that if I thought I could, I could.

ACKNOWLEDGEMENTS

Though my name alone appears on the cover, please add these people whose work and support have made this book a reality:

Debra Lindland, for her cover design and all illustrations;

Jeff Levin of Pendragon Graphics, for his excellent book design counsel, typesetting, and editing;

writer Bill Woodall, whose brilliant idea it was to dictate my first draft;

Judy Binder, for transcribing my audio cassette dictation and for editing. Barbara Kemph for proofreading;

Joseph Photographer, for a complimentary author photograph;

Jim Cole, 21st Century Graphics, for the graphics;

Dan Poynter, whose publishing advice continues to guide me;

readers and critiquers Betsy Bolding, Doug Crane, and Mary Jane Pelson;

my clients, whose needs and whose successes enable me to continue to grow;

and my husband, Kent Franklin, for his love, support, and encouragement.

CONTENTS— BRIEF VERSION

CONTENTS

CHAPTER TWO 35

PLANNING IS THE KEY TO SUCCESS

CHAPTER THREE 53

CREATING THE OPENER

CHAPTER FOUR 63

INVOLVING THE AUDIENCE

CHAPTER FIVE 73

DEVELOPING THE STRUCTURE

CHAPTER SIX 79

DEVELOPING THE CONTENT

CHAPTER SEVEN 89

PLANNING TEAM PRESENTATIONS

CHAPTER EIGHT 103

PREPARING EFFECTIVE VISUALS

CHAPTER NINE   117

PREPARING BEFORE THE PRESENTATION

CHAPTER TEN   133

PREPARING YOUR MIND— MINIMIZE YOUR NERVOUSNESS

INTRODUCTION

Why master the SKILL of public speaking? Two compelling reasons: to become more **powerful** and to have more **fun**.

What about being **powerful**? The *American Heritage Dictionary* defines *power* as "the ability or capacity to act or perform effectively." Every time you are in front of a group one of your primary goals is to perform effectively, so the act of public speaking itself is powerful. Speakers have power; GREAT speakers have GREAT power.

To tap that power in you, you first need good ideas and confidence in those ideas. Beyond those qualities, think of being effective as a three-step process: get people's attention, keep their attention long enough for them to listen, and get them to change or to act. All three of those tasks can often be accomplished in one step through a speech or presentation. You have a captive audience.

The audience generally knows in advance what your subject will be. People are usually present because they want to be. Because you are in charge, others are ready to be led; because you are prepared, others can grasp your message easily; because your delivery is dynamic, others are drawn to what you say. That's power!

What about having **fun**? To speak is to perform. To speak is to persuade others to your idea, to get action for your cause. It is also often to enchant, to entrance, to entertain. The natural high that successful speakers feel equals the high that entertainers and athletes feel after a successful performance. This feeling of elation and satisfaction is also power!

Maximizing the power you can command as a speaker is a life-long process. At whatever point you are in that process, resolve TODAY to grow.

Growth can be an informal process as well as a formal one.

Informally, watch, listen and read:

- Whenever you attend speeches, watch the speakers. Let part of your mind observe and learn from both the good and the poor speakers. Watch their gestures and posture; note their enthusiasm and credibility.
- Listen to announcers, hosts, and guests on radio and television programs to learn more about the effective use of the voice. Pay attention to use of pauses.
- Notice visuals in your reading. Visuals in print media can broaden your understanding of how visuals catch people's attention. (Television is a full-time lesson in visuals to supplement words.)

Make a **formal** commitment to become a competent speaker:

- Sign up for speech communications classes at your local college or night school program.
- Join a Toastmaster's Club.
- Start a small speaker's support group with colleagues or friends.
- Accept opportunities to speak on behalf of your recreational, social, or civic organizations.

In other words, **SPEAK**. Be **powerful** and have **fun!**

—Marian K. Woodall

SPEAKING TO A GROUP

**Mastering the SKILL
of public speaking**

CHAPTER ONE

PUBLIC SPEAKING IS A SKILL AND YOU CAN MASTER IT

The most significant word on the cover of this book is the word *skill*, because public speaking is a skill. If you have been one of those people who has long dreaded trying to be a better presenter or who has felt, "I can't present, I'm a terrible speaker," you need to understand that public speaking is a skill. Why is that important? Because it is a skill, you can take specific steps to master this skill in the same way that you have learned to master other skills. Think about one or two activities that you do very well—whether it's golf, tennis, baking soufflés, making pies, knitting, arranging flowers—whatever it is that you do that you are very proud of, that you do extremely well. How did you get to be good at it?

If you remember, you probably took some lessons or learned by watching someone you knew who did a good job at that activity. You picked up some tips, some strategies, in one way or another, and then you practiced, and practiced, and practiced. You performed that skill day after day, week after week, year after year. Finally, as often happens with us, one day you examined that skill and you thought, "Well, I'm good at this!" That same process is the process that you can go through using this book to learn the skill of public speaking.

A second significant aspect about the cover of this book is the word *speaking*. This term means all kinds of communications that you would do with a few people or many people in a situation where you want to do something more than just have a simple conversation.

Speaking to a group means many different kinds of communicating. You may think of it as public speaking, or lecturing, or presenting, or giving a talk, or even selling. Whatever you call it, please remember that we are talking about any basic communication situation in which you wish to have more impact than just a conversation.

What constitutes speaking to a group, then, can be a tremendous variety of communications activities. You might, for example, be making a presentation to your boss about something you would like to have different about your job. You would not necessarily think of that as a speech, but you do recognize that you want it to be something more significant than simply conversation. You want to have impact. You want to have a little flair. You want to have something special about your words, about your delivery of those words, about your presentation of those words, that will give you the edge that you need, that will allow you to feel, sound, and look confident, professional, in control.

Sales activities (whether you present to one prospective client, or several individuals from a given firm) are also speaking to a group, also presentations, because you have a specific goal. Making a committee report, giving a talk to a professional organization, speaking to a social or civic organization, doing some training, presenting a formal speech to an evening group—all of these situations constitute speaking to a group. They constitute a presentation.

There are two distinctions which separate speaking from conversation: a planned, specific goal and a speaker who is standing. The first distinction in speaking to a group which makes it different from a conversation is that you have the goal of getting someone to hear you and understand and perhaps to accept what you have to say. Acceptance is not a requirement, but understanding is certainly one of your goals.

STAND WHEN PRESENTING

Another distinction in a speaking situation is that in most all cases you will be standing and your audience will be seated. If your reaction is, "Hey, I wouldn't want to stand in front of my boss," or "I wouldn't want to stand in front of my potential customer if he's just sitting at a table," my response to you is, "Of course, you would," **if** you want to be successful. Delivery skills are discussed throughout, (especially in Chapters Eleven and Twelve), but standing to present is so important that you need to see yourself standing from the beginning.

Speaking while standing gives you many advantages over speaking while you are seated. The first of those is a sense of presence, a sense in yourself and in your audience, that what you have to say is important. Second, it gives you an opportunity for better delivery. You will use your delivery instruments—your voice and your body—more effectively. Your voice will be firmer and more authoritative, your gestures will be larger and more emphatic. In a conversation you typically use a normal voice, some limited gestures (especially if you are standing!), and your face; when you are standing you will have full use of your instruments.

PRESENTING—
AN IMPORTANT SKILL TO MASTER

Why is presenting an important skill? Of all the ways you can enhance both your personal and professional self, being able to make presentations is, I believe, the most important single way. Presenting is the most important single tool that you can add to your repertoire of professional and personal skills.

Why? First of all, the process of developing and focusing ideas that you must go through to present effectively helps you to understand what it is you believe; this process helps you to articulate your concepts and thoughts by forcing you to come to terms with them in the rather specific ways we will be talking about in Chapter Two. Trust me on this: As a professor, speech coach, and professional speaker myself, I can say with certainty that once you have wrestled with the information that you wish to communicate sufficiently to get the one sentence thesis that you need, you will have a much stronger, more positive and more controlled feeling about your idea, concept, or belief.

Next, presenting enables you to share with other people what you think is important. Presenting enables you to get listeners for ideas that you feel are significant. Presenting enables you to find other people whom you believe will care about the same thing that you care about.

Third, presenting is an important skill because you can demonstrate to the people around you that you have added value. Your ability to volunteer, to offer to make presentations within your firm, within your profession, to customers and potential customers, to your civic organizations, allows you the opportunity to enhance your position in your life and in your world.

Being competent in speaking to a group is a wonderful tool to have when you are seeking promotions, when you are seeking additional opportunities to get exposure in your firm, to get additional exposure in your civic group, cause, or profession.

FEAR OF PUBLIC SPEAKING

You probably know that fear of public speaking is considered by many the number one phobia in the United States. There is absolutely no reason, in my mind, for that phobia to continue to be so widespread. Because public speaking is a skill, it is something you can master. There are ways to get over the fear, ways to change that part of your life. Because speaking is a learned skill, most everyone can become a competent speaker.

While there may not be an easy way to change a fear of heights, or a fear of snakes, there is an easy way to get over the fear of public speaking. The secret is to change your attitude. Begin now to refocus your attitude about presenting.

As a speech coach, I have frequently heard clients and prospective clients, say, "I'm a terrible speaker." My reaction to them? "I'll bet you are." After they have looked in astonishment at me for having said such a terrible thing, I add, "Simply thinking that you are a poor speaker is one of the most common self-fulfilling prophecies. If you said it to me, you probably have said it a hundred or a thousand times. Every time you say something such as that, you in fact reinforce the feeling, reinforce the inadequacy, reinforce the lack of confidence. Naturally you are going to be unsuccessful; you just programmed yourself to be unsuccessful!" There's an old saying that whether you think you're going to be good at it or not, you're always right. You **can** master the skill of speaking to a group. Mastering begins **now**, and it must begin with you. It begins in your head. You must begin to say, right this moment, "This is a skill that I can acquire. I can be a good public speaker. I can be a confident presenter."

These are affirmations. Using affirmations is a well-known method of helping people to succeed at a task. The focus of an affirmation is to phrase what you want to become and to say it as many times as you need to, to help that concept become a part of a new pattern of thinking. Say your affirmation sentences frequently—out loud. Say them when you're in the shower, driving to work, waiting for a stop light, jogging, or out for a walk.

Another common approach in self-improvement is visualizing. Visualizing has received much publicity in sports psychology since the last Olympics. Visualizing can also help in your quest to overcome fear and master the skill of public speaking. Visualize yourself successfully completing a public speaking situation. See yourself actually walking to the front of the room, making eye contact with the audience, delivering your powerful first sentence. Visualize yourself doing the entire speech right through to the end where the audience leaps to its feet in spontaneous applause for your wonderful words and your dynamic delivery. (See Chapter Ten for more on affirmations and visualization.)

PRESENTING IS COMMUNICATING

Presenting is communicating, and as I indicated earlier, one difference between presentation and conversation is essentially a matter of delivery—that you are standing, rather than seated; that your voice is stronger and firmer; that your gestures are larger and more emphatic. However, what you do with any other conversational situation is what you can do in speaking to a group.

Here's an exercise that you can practice, not only to discover that presenting is, in fact, just BIGGER communicating, but also one which will help you understand that there is no need to be fearful of speaking to groups. For this exercise you will need to gather at least five or six friends, colleagues, or peers to help. Go into a room with just one person. Your role is to tell that person— without interruption since it is a presentation and not a conversation—a story or something else that you feel comfortable or strongly about. That person may be standing or seated. You should be standing.

You will have asked the other people waiting outside to come in to join you at two-minute intervals. As you are speaking to your one colleague, a second colleague will come in to join her as your audience. You continue speaking in the very same way. A third person will come in and stand or sit nearby. What you discover that you do, without realizing it and without any training, is to simply adjust your body slightly so you can include the other person into your field of vision, into your voice range.

As people add themselves to the audience, you will find that your voice gets bigger and more dramatic; your gestures become larger and a bit more emphatic. To complete the exercise, keep adding people.

You will be amazed and astounded and, I hope, gratified to realize that you continued to speak naturally as the audience got bigger with no changes other than those slight adjustments to your body position and your gestures. And you will have changed those aspects naturally to accommodate the growing audience.

Remember what it's like at a large social gathering? You are chatting, glass or appetizer in hand, with one other individual. As you begin to tell a story, someone else comes up to join you. You smile a welcome and turn your body to include him, but you keep talking. Another person comes because she's heard this excitement or laughter coming from your group. And so on and so on, until finally, there is a little knot of people around you and you are reveling in this story that you're telling. You are presenting. It is as simple as that. You are presenting.

WHY PLAN?

When you know a topic, you can communicate naturally and comfortably. Picture yourself on a long flight in an airplane. You've finished your book, you've already read the airline magazine — you're bored. The person sitting next to you looks all right, so you decide to strike up a conversation. You ask her what she does, and she responds briefly. She then asks you a question about your work. Do you say, "I'd love to tell you about my work. Let me go to the back of the plane and spend a few minutes getting a little outline together, and then I'll be happy to tell you about my work"? Of course you don't. You simply start to talk. You talk out of your knowledge, your enthusiasm, your expertise about your subject. The person sitting next to you gives you feedback — nods, smiles, asks questions to help you to help her to understand the details.

During the course of the conversation, you probably say enough of the things that you need to say or want to say in order to help this person understand what you are about in your profession. You don't necessarily put it in any certain order, but by the time you've finished, you have completed the "presentation." If you can do that, if you can tell someone in a social situation what you do and how it works — without any preplanning or any thought or any organizing — can't you do the same thing in front of a group of people? You can, with only two added steps.

When your intent is to speak to a group you typically need to add two things to the communication process. First, you verbally include some structure or organization to help the audience follow you; second, you plan what you are going to say with the specific audience in mind. You might be thinking, "If communicating is so natural, why plan?" When the audience gets larger, organizing the material makes it flow better and makes it easy to follow. It's harder to get accompanying feedback from a group than from an individual. You plan and organize a presentation so that the audience can help you to succeed.

POINTS TO REMEMBER

Reflect upon your ability to tell people in conversation what you know about and care about. Try the add-one-at-a-time audience exercise. You will be reaffirmed and reassured that you do communicate. Presenting is communicating. If you can communicate, you can master speaking to a group.

The TO DO List:

List specific situations in your work, your professional, civic, volunteer, and community service in which speaking to a group may be possible or necessary. Beside each, note the potential for enhancing yourself if you say "yes" to an opportunity to speak.

Resolve to say "YES"!

CHAPTER TWO

PLANNING IS THE KEY TO SUCCESS

Developing a speech is a process. The word *process* suggests that there are steps or phases to be dealt with, that the steps have a logical order, and that once those steps are completed, the process will be finished. Most of this process is the same whether you are going to prepare a talk to deliver extemporaneously (with notes) or as a manuscript presentation or lecture.

DEVELOPING THE PRESENTATION

There are four distinct phases to consider in preparing a presentation:

- Prepare the content—both material and structure (Chapters Three–Six).

- Prepare your instruments—your mind, your voice, and your body (Chapters Ten–Twelve).
- Prepare your visual aids (Chapters Eight and Thirteen).
- Prepare the room and the equipment (Chapter Nine).

(If you are presenting with other people, a fifth key area is co-ordinating the team effort. See Chapter Seven).

The key to success is found in the first area: the assessment and planning you do before the presentation. There are many reasons why this aspect is the most significant, as you will discover. The most important reason is that the more that you can do to get ready for something ahead of time, the better prepared you're going to be when you actually do it. It's like doing homework before an exam. It's like having your report written, typed, and bound before you approach the client. It's like making sure that your clothes are pressed, your make-up is great, your tie is straight, before you go to a meeting. You are confident about everything you have taken care of ahead of time; you have less to be concerned about during the actual presentation. You can focus your attention on delivering the message.

ASSESSING YOUR AUDIENCE

The key to all planning and preparation is making certain that the material you will present is appropriate to your specific audience. Audience appropriateness is **everything**. In fact, the only part of the presentation that comes from your own perspective is the fact that you have enough information or background to be giving the presentation. Everything else is planned from the perspective of the audience. It's not what could be said to these people, it's what **should** be said to them. It's not what you want them to know, it's what they are willing to hear, what they want to hear, or what they will sit still for. Failure to understand this essential truth that everything comes from the perspective of the audience is—in my experiences as a professional speaker, as a speech coach, and as a teacher of speech—the biggest single error made in public speaking, from sale presentations to staff morale speeches, from fund raisers to awards ceremonies. As a simple way to see the way this orientation to the perspective of the audience changes the way you present, consider the language of a situation in which the old-style speaker said, "We can't finish your file until we receive the additional information we need." Now, from the perspective of the audience: "As soon as you send us the additional information we need, your file can be finished." The change from *we* to *you* makes all the difference in the world.

On a recent visit to New York, I sat in as my client presented his prepared remarks in dry run as preparation for an international public stock offering. The audience at the dry run was a group of investment bankers and stock analysts—individuals from the two firms which were handling my client's upcoming offering. Their input was directed at fine-tuning the phrasing and the examples to meet the ears of the final audience: investors. These comments were typical: "That's what investors want to hear . . ." and "They don't care about . . ." and "That's the kind of language that will get the attention of investors." What my client wanted to tell was not as important as what the investors would be interested in hearing.

How do you ascertain what the appropriate material is? First, know precisely and in detail who the audience is. In many cases, you know exactly who's going to be in the audience. In other cases, you will need to find out who the audience will be. Then you assess that audience to prepare material which is focused and presented from their perspective.

Use this triangle to begin your assessment:

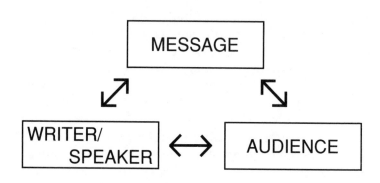

The Communications Triangle
© 1979, Marian K. Woodall

As you assess the communications triangle, ask yourself these questions:

- Who is this audience?
- Who am I in relation to this audience?
- What is the general message that needs to be communicated to this audience?
- What is my relationship to the message?
- What is the audience's relationship to the message?
- How do all these aspects relate, and what do these relationships tell me about the way I should approach my material?

Using a worksheet, begin to answer these questions. First, jot down all the things you know about the audience — what is their likely age range, and education or background? Is it a board, a committee, a group of professionals, people from the same firm, people from different firms with similar jobs, people from the same firm with the same jobs? Classmates taking an elective course? People with the same avocation or hobby? In other words, everything you can think of about that audience. The more you know about them, the better you will be able to relate to them as real people who want and need to hear your message, the better you will present material that they can respond to. Get to know the perspectives of that audience.

Answer the question: Who am I in relationship to that audience? Are you first among equals? The expert? A colleague in the same firm? A professional colleague in the same industry? The boss? A subordinate who's speaking to the board of directors? An engineer speaking to marketing people? A marketing person speaking to data processing people? A member speaking to fellow members? The more you can discover about your relationship to that audience, including how you perceive them and how they're apt to perceive you, the better you're going to be able to tailor your message to a perspective they will understand and accept.

The other legs of the communications triangle need the same kind of assessment. Who am I in relationship to this message? Am I being asked by someone else to present? Am I the person who originated all the ideas? Am I simply the bearer of information? Am I the persuader? Am I the person who is trying to obtain action on something? Figure out how you relate to that message.

Continue your assessment by writing down as much as you can about how your audience relates to this message. Are they looking forward to it? Are they dreading it? Do they know the background? Do they have an understanding of why it's important? Have they gotten similar messages in the past? Is the message going to help them be richer or smarter or do their work better? Is it going to be painful for them? Is it going to be expensive for them? And so on.

THE TWO PERCENT RULE

It is these assessments that will enable you to decide what material is going to go into the presentation and what will be left out. Left out, you say? Yes, left out. The single most common error in presentations, in my twenty years' experience as a speech trainer, is that speakers try to give too much information. They try to say too much. They try to tell the audience everything they know. Consider the **Two Percent Rule**, and let it be the guide for your presentation strategies: in a presentation of an hour or less, you will typically present no more than 2% of what you know about the topic.

That's good news. The reason it's good news is that if you present 2%, you have 98% left in reserve to help you in case the situation gets difficult or your mind goes blank or you forget something when you're answering questions. Having 98% in reserve is another edge of confidence that helps you know that you can do a superb job.

Contrast this rule of thumb (2% presentation, 98% in reserve) to what it was like when you took the speech class in high school or college. You typically went to the library and found an encyclopedia (plus one other book or article) from which you quickly scribbled down as many notes as you could to fill the five-minute speech that you had to prepare. You got up to give your speech.

You had the five minutes plus an additional fifteen seconds' worth. That is, you presented 98% of what you knew. You had nothing in reserve.

What's significant about that situation is that you had to write lots of notes on your note cards (or you had the whole speech written out) because you had to present everything you knew; you couldn't afford to forget anything. However, following the Two Percent Rule, as a professional or an adult speaker, you know that there is a great deal that you might say; you're going to choose the 2% that is most appropriate given your assessment of the communications triangle. What your assessments help you to discern is what a particular audience needs to hear, or wants to hear, or will sit still for — the 2% that will help you get your point across.

Until you have done the assessment of the triangle, there is no way that you can determine the appropriate 2%. You have to decide how much background to give, how much explanation to give, how many benefits to sell, how many features to describe, how much explanation is needed.

In addition to doing the worksheet for assessing the audience and your relationship to it, you also want to begin thinking about the topic in your spare moments. It's important to get as much material as you can out of your head and onto paper. Once ideas and thoughts are onto paper, you can look at them, analyze them, assess them, and use them. You don't have to remember them. You don't have to try to keep juggling it all in your mind. When a thought occurs to you, jot it down — on a yellow sticky note, on a cocktail napkin, on a piece of scratch paper. Put these jottings in a folder.

You never start with a blank sheet or a blank screen. Take advantage of the thought processes that you can go through when you're out for a walk, swimming your laps, in the shower, driving to and from work or meetings.

Jot down as soon as you can the thoughts that occur to you; you get a tremendous amount of thinking done, much of the material gathered, and quite a bit of planning taken care of, without using any extra time or taking any time out of your normal day. Actually sitting down to prepare the presentation is comfortable because you have so much of the raw material assembled.

DEFINE YOUR PURPOSE

Now you have all of this assessment done, notes taken, and ideas gathered, what's the next step? Define your purpose. Though there are many different kinds of presentations that you might give, there are five basic purposes, one of which will eventually be identified as your primary purpose:

- inform
- teach or instruct
- educate
- convince or persuade
- get action.

Though it is true that you may have more than one of those purposes as a part of the material of the presentation, your ultimate purpose, your goal, must be clearly identified in your own mind as one of these five. You must have a single purpose in mind, because it is not possible to accomplish several of them in a single speech. A common error that people make when presenting is trying to accomplish too much. They have too complex a purpose or too ambitious a goal.

Consider these purposes one at a time. First of all, to **inform**. To inform is to pass along information, statistics, data, or opinions, to a group of people. That's the most difficult kind of speech to give because the potential for boredom is high (for both the audience and the speaker). If you look at the communications triangle assessment and you are certain that all you're going to do is inform, my strong suggestion is to send a memo, send a letter, or write a short report. It's difficult to stay interesting as a speaker, and it's equally difficult to stay interested as an audience in most situations when the purpose is just to inform.

If your purpose is to **teach or instruct**, you are usually going to give more than 2%. To **educate** an audience is generally less detailed and often more theoretical than instructing them. In both cases you have ready-made a particular approach to the material. Your assessment of the audience will help you determine the level of language and the organizational approach that will be helpful.

If your goal is to **convince or persuade**, your own feelings are strong (though not always clear) at the beginning. You recognize the nature of language that you need to use, the kind of spin that you wish to put on the phrases or concepts, to get the audience to understand, to agree, to be moved by what you say.

If your primary purpose is to **get action**, the bottom line is that you must say, especially at the end, exactly what you want them to do. "Send your check today." "Sign up for this wonderful seminar." "Write your congressman." "Write a letter to the newspaper."

Go back to the worksheet, consider your assessments, and decide your one major purpose.

Many people feel, especially in social action situations, that they must convince and get action at the same time. Some speakers see these two goals as inseparable. It is extremely difficult to achieve both in one speech because convincing is one process, and getting action as a result of people's convictions is another process entirely. Different motivations are present. If you are in a situation prepared to give a presentation where this is absolutely, positively the only opportunity that you will ever have with these people, then you have to think carefully: Do I want to try to convince them and then try to get them to take some action as a result of that change of mind? Should I just try to convince them and hope that they'll take some action on their own? Shall I go right for the "get action" purpose and hope that my material is compelling enough to move most of them to that action position?

CREATE YOUR ONE-SENTENCE THESIS

The next clearly defined aspect of planning your presentation is narrowing the focus down to that 2% — that one-sentence thesis or focus. You must be able to say in just one sentence exactly what you want the audience to take away with them from your presentation. Remember your high school or college English composition classes where the instructor insisted that you write a thesis sentence **before** you began your composition? You thought it was a stupid thing to have to do. You wanted to just start writing. Just starting to write is not very successful, primarily because it requires you to write too much.

You are writing (or planning, in the case of public speaking) in order to figure out what it is you want to say. Much better to do the process by **thinking** about what it is you want to say in your head and on paper during the assessment. Then you can work at creating the single sentence, which is the thesis or the focus.

Once you have it, planning the rest of the presentation is usually quite simple.

It's quite simple because you are forcing yourself to wrestle with all of what you know and distill it to what you need to say in this presentation in order to reach this audience with the purpose that you have in mind. If you need to write a long sentence or two sentences or three sentences, just keep cutting away at it, keep pruning it, until you get it down to one concise, pithy, dynamite sentence. That forces you to narrow the focus, forces you to reduce the material down to the heart of your message. It forces you to find the 2%.

If your goal is to have the audience leave with a particular message, you owe it to them to have that message as concisely prepared as you can. If you can't get it in one sentence, the chances are virtually certain that it's not going to be clear enough, concise enough, simple enough for the audience to grasp what it is you want them to grasp. In fact, the entire presentation, not just the thesis statement, needs to be so clear and simple — to your mind — that you are close to feeling embarrassed about the simplicity. The reason for such simplicity is obvious: you are the expert, you have wrestled with the material and the sentence extensively. If it doesn't seem almost too clear and simple to you, with all this work behind you, what chance does an audience have, hearing it just once? If you doubt the wisdom of such simplicity, answer this one question? When was the last time you heard a presentation that was too clear and too simple? Ha! It doesn't happen much, does it?

If you have trouble wrestling with the one sentence, in fact, if you have trouble in any part of this planning process, ask someone to sit in with you. Ask a colleague, someone in your family, a member of your organization, a classmate, to brainstorm with you in assessment of the audience, the message, the purpose. All of this process can be made simpler and easier, not to mention more interesting, by talking with someone. Two heads are truly better than one, and someone who is asking you questions can force you to be clear in your thinking rather than muddle-headed, can add insights that perhaps you had not thought of, can help you bring things to the surface of your consciousness about the topic that otherwise may not surface as quickly (sometimes not at all). In fact, ask someone to brainstorm with you at any aspect of the presentation where you are not moving as rapidly as you would like.

Your goal at this point is to have a one-sentence statement, which is the heart and soul of your presentation. In most instances your thesis will be precise, narrow, and specific, with an organizational plan which contains sometimes broad and sometimes more specific support material. However, consider the option of a thesis that is a broad truth or universal belief which you support with two or three individual examples or illustrations. The commonality of the examples can support the universality or generality of the thesis.

These are instances when, as it is said, the examples prove the rule. A government employee asked for my assistance in preparing a twenty-minute presentation for a national audience which was an update on a new set of three different programs that she was instrumental in developing for several different regions around the U.S. The officials for the conference had thoughtfully provided her with a list of items to be covered, a gigantic list of stuff! She and I quickly agreed that such a presentation, "reporting on all the items on the list for each program for every region" would be deadly dull. We drew up a broad thesis highlighting the excitement of change, with three main points, one for each program. The body of the speech, the support material, would consist of one real life success story for each of the three programs. She could thus include at least three of the regions specifically. Her ability to relate stories would add sparkle and vigor to the presentation; the enthusiasm of success stories insured a dynamite presentation!

SELECT THE STRUCTURE—
THE ORGANIZATIONAL PATTERN

Your next major decision is the structure of the presentation—the organizational pattern. The content of a speech has two parts, the structure and the material. Selecting an organizational plan is one step in creating the structure. (Developing oral guidelines is the other; see Chapter Five.)

There are five basic organizational patterns:

- Topical
- Chronological
- Spatial
- Problem solving
- Need-fulfillment.

If you have a good thesis, and you have in mind some points to support it, what you have is a **topical** organizational plan. A topical plan, such as the government conference example above, includes three or four logical divisions of your thesis, individual topics that relate to the thesis that are of generally equal importance and value. That's one basic, common organizational plan for development of a topic. It's the structure that most speeches are prepared in: three divisions of the company, four parts of the re-organization plan, two phases of development, three parts of the recovery plan.

Four other common organizational plans will be useful for you at some time in your presentations. Number two, a **chronological** development plan, uses a time frame or a time line, beginning in the past, talking about the present, and then the future; beginning with the opening days of a project, continuing through the second phase, and on to the final phase; the before and after of a particular project; the "how we used to do it" compared to "how we do it now"; six steps in order to complete the project—all of those are aspects of the chronological development plan. If you have a chronological topic, it will be obvious to you that this is the appropriate organization pattern to take. And you're lucky because that kind of presentation organizes itself.

The third organizational plan is **spatial**. This plan is for physical items or geographic locations. Its structure presents material from the front to the back, from the top to the bottom, from the left-hand side to the right-hand side, from California to New York, from the inside to the outside. Physical items or geographic location topics which lend themselves to spatial organization are also nice to have because in most cases there is a logical order. If there does not appear to be a logical order, that is, if the items or locations could be talked about in any order, then you go back to the perspective of your audience and decide which order would be most logical from their perspective. It's not what will make sense to you that matters, it's what will make sense to this audience. Once again, you are back to your assessment of the audience in the communications triangle.

The fourth organizational plan for development is **problem solving**. For this organizational plan, you first demonstrate that a problem exists, you next attribute the causes, and you then propose a solution. This becomes a three-part presentation. Many times the problem demonstration part is not necessary in detail because the audience knows that part as well as you do. Assessment of the triangle will indicate that this first phase can be safely included in the 98% that gets left out.

The fifth organizational plan is **need-fulfillment**. In the first part of your presentation you either create a need or desire or you describe a need or desire that the audience already has. In the second part, you propose a method to fulfill that need. This, of course, is a common organizational plan for sales reps. Knowledge of your audience is important in order to accurately describe the need or desire. Knowledge of your product is important to propose a method to fulfill it, but you are careful to describe the fulfillment in terms of benefits to the audience, not in terms of features of the product or service.

One of these five organizational plans will usually be the appropriate plan. Seventy-five percent of basic presentations are topical. A topical organization is hardest, only because it's the most difficult topic to narrow down to the 2%. There are many things that you might say, and you must keep constantly asking yourself, "Who's the audience? What's in this for them?" "Of all the things I might say, what are the things that they need to hear?" If your approach turns out to be topical, work to narrow and distill and reduce until you are sure that you have the right two, three, or four oral guidelines, the main support points.

This plan provides the structure of your presentation. Having this structure is important because it lets you know that you're in control. It also guides all the rest of your presentation, including expanding these support points and creating your visual aids. Another wonderful aspect of having the structure in hand is that you have your "elevator" speech prepared. You find yourself standing next to the decision-maker in the elevator, with the ride time of ten floors to make your point. If you have the thesis and your support points, you can make the most of the elevator ride! Or you expect to make your pitch in front of the group in a calm, well-timed presentation; what is apt to happen is that the key individual comes up to you beforehand with this comment, "I'm going to miss your presentation, Jane. Give me the highlights." Or you get to your appointed place and the chairperson says, "Oh, I'm sorry, we're running terribly behind. We've only got five minutes for you instead of the fifteen we promised you. Will that be all right?" You'll be able to say, "Of course," because you have the essence of what you want to say, and you can deliver those four sentences very easily, with great impact, great emphasis. The extra ten minutes that you were going to use was simply material to draw the audience to your topic. It's wonderful to have that extra ten or twenty minutes, of course, but once you have the essence in hand, you will never be thrown off by someone who says, as they frequently do, "You don't have as much time as we thought you had. Please be brief."

SUMMARY

Here is a short summary of questions to ask yourself as you are ready to prepare a speech:

First, what is the one sentence that tells the essence of my message? By the way, note that the sentence is apt to change as you go along. That's fine, what you want is a working thesis, but if you can't write it in one sentence, you aren't ready to prepare.

Secondly, what is the major purpose of the presentation — to inform; to educate, to train or instruct; to persuade or convince or build good will; to get action; and are you looking for general action or specific action?

Remember, that to inform only generally requires a very high degree of technical information, an especially innovative concept or some equally specialized piece of knowledge in order to be an interesting presentation. To use informing as the basis of support for another one of the focuses is a more typical approach.

Number three, what two or three major points validate or support that thesis sentence? How are those key points of support related to each other? Some of those points may become sub-points as you are wrestling with the support material. It is difficult to try to get more than three points across.

Note—If you have more than three major points, the chances are that you need more work on the material. You either have two speeches or else you haven't refined the material enough.

Number four, do these major points suit the purpose of my presentation? At this point, you must be conscious of the need to rephrase the key points and even rephrase the thesis sentence as many times as is necessary to get the fit that you want.

POINTS TO REMEMBER

Preparing a speech is a process. The more work you do in your mind ahead of time the less work you will have to do in preparation. Planning is the key to success.

The TO DO List:

Make a list of some past talks you have given. Examine each briefly:

- Did I assess my audience and meet their needs (or did I mostly meet my own)?
- Did I have a central idea? Did I express it in one sentence during the presentation? (Dig out your notes or outlines if you need to.)

CHAPTER THREE

CREATING THE OPENER

Once you have the planning completed, you have amassed a good deal of material, notes, ideas, concepts, and you are ready to actually create your presentation. There are five—only five—features absolutely necessary for success in developing good presentations:

- An effective introduction (Chapters Three and Four).
- Careful oral guidelines (Chapter Five).
- Good graphics or visuals (Chapter Eight).
- Details, briefly but specifically (Chapter Six).
- A good close (Chapter Six).

Though there are other aspects that we will be concerned about in this book, if you develop these five features carefully for your presentation, the content will be a success. It is as simple as that. This chapter will cover developing the first part of a good introduction: the opener.

GOALS OF AN EFFECTIVE INTRODUCTION

The first material in your presentation is the introduction. The introduction establishes everything — topic, focus, mood, tone. No matter what organizational plan you choose, the introduction is composed of these four parts: the opener, an involvement device or activity (if separate from the opener), the thesis statement, and the oral guidelines. Openers are discussed in Chapter Three; involvement devices in Chapter Four; identifying the central idea and developing oral guidelines in Chapter Five.

First, consider the goals of an effective introduction:

- Get the audience's attention.
- Involve the audience.
- Identify your central idea.
- Name major points with oral guidelines.

GET THE AUDIENCE'S ATTENTION— THE OPENER

The first words out of your mouth when you stand up to speak, the first sentence of the introduction, is the opener. The opener is the key to the introduction because it will get your audience's attention. Consider the opener a hook to catch or capture the minds of the audience. When you begin to give a presentation, no matter where you're speaking or what kind of group it is, only one person in the room has his or her mind fully on the topic of the day—you. Everyone else is thinking about something else—how hot it is, how much work she has set aside to come to the session, what to do about his sick child, how to handle her angry boss, what to say to his irritated spouse. Everybody's mind is somewhere else.

Your opener is the key to moving those minds away from their thoughts and onto your topic. Usually, that means that the opener will consist of words directly related to your material. Often, in fact, it will be your tightly crafted thesis sentence. However, other options exist.

Here are seven basic possibilities for openers:

- a clear thesis
- a question
- an autobiographical comment
- a statistic
- a quotation
- a dramatic or vital statement
- a descriptive opener.

You can never go wrong by beginning with your carefully developed **thesis sentence**—especially if you deliver it powerfully. It is the one sentence that you want the audience to take away with them; it's well crafted, it's precise and exact, you know it so well you can deliver it with great dynamism and great enthusiasm. It's a wonderful opener.

However, you may choose some other hook to get the audience's attention, to arouse their curiosity, to get them involved in some way; you can always follow that hook with your clear thesis.

Option number two, a **question**, is my personal favorite for the hook because, since it is phrased in the second person, it forces the audience to think about the subject of the question just for a second. "Do you ever . . . ?" "How many of you have . . . ?" "Are you willing to . . . ?" This kind of opener forces mental involvement. Individuals in the audience may think, "I'm not going to think about that," but it's too late. You've already hooked them.

It is also effective to ask a series of questions, provided that they meet these criteria: they are closely related, they are brief, and they are delivered with appropriate timing (enough pause after each for the audience to think about the question, but not such a long pause that they lose track of the series).

How about number three, an **autobiographical comment**? There are both good things and bad things to be said about using an autobiographical comment. Think about this device carefully and then use it carefully, because it is easy to make the autobiographical comment too long, easy for it to become boring. We all like to talk about ourselves. It's tempting to get so involved in telling about ourselves that we lose perspective.

On the other hand an autobiographical comment lets the audience know something about you, helps them to identify with you. If it is important that they know some things about you because of your position relative to the message or because of what you're going to ask them to do, then sharing details about yourself right off the top can be a great help. For example, you might begin an address to a professional group of consultants this way: "I've just completed my tenth year as a management consultant, and I've learned one lesson over all: being an expert is hard work!"

A **statistic**, a **quotation**, a **dramatic or vital statement** all fall in the same category—something to jolt people, something to startle them. Your hook engages their minds because of the immensity of the number, because of the tremendous quality of the quotation, because of the gripping nature of the vital statement.

I remember as an undergraduate at the University of Idaho many years ago being invited to a presentation by an environmentalist. In the early 1960s, we didn't even know what an environmentalist was. We did not know what to expect from this speaker.

He strode into the room, up to the table in front of where we nine students were seated, opened his mouth, and intoned in a slow, deep, resonant voice, "Within twenty years, three out of the ten people in this room will be dead from the effects of environmental pollution." You can believe that he got our attention. We all began to think, "Am I going to be one of the three?" (He did exactly the right thing in terms of delivery, and that was a long, long pause to let that statement, and that statistic, soak in.) As he went on to give the rest of his presentation, he had us literally in the palm of his hand.

How can you pick a question, a statistic, a quotation, a vital statement which will be appropriate for your audience? Because you have assessed them carefully, you understand what will motivate them, you can find an effective hook, a dramatic or involving sentence which will get them to the mental place where you want them to be—receptive to what you have to say.

The seventh opening idea, a **descriptive opener**, is fun to do if you have some imagination and can develop a scene (either real or imagined) with descriptive language. Begin a descriptive opener by saying, "Imagine that you're seated at your desk. It's ten o'clock at night. Everyone is gone from the office. The whole building is dark and cold except your one single little office; the glow of your green computer screen provides the only warmth in the room."

You might begin a descriptive opener by saying, "Visualize . . ." Or, you might describe something that you have seen, a place that you have been, a situation that you've been involved in. The key here is description: Make it interesting, make it lively and visual so the audience gets a sharp mental picture as you are talking. Place them in the scene.

WHAT ABOUT JOKES?

Notice that there is not an opener called a joke. There is not an opener called a joke because jokes are generally not successful openers. You know this. You have heard speakers tell jokes that embarrassed you, affronted you, offended your dignity, that made you or someone else in the audience downright angry. You've heard jokes that didn't come off, after which there was a pained silence. The audience was discomforted for the speaker. The speaker was discomforted for himself. There are so many problems with telling a joke and so few things right about it, that I recommend never using jokes as openers unless you are a professional humorist.

What is wrong with jokes as openers? First, jokes generally depend for their humor on making fun of somebody or something; it's extremely difficult to tell a joke which does not insult someone in your audience. You can't afford to risk that. The second reason that jokes are inappropriate is that they are seldom related closely enough to your material that you can transition into the speech after you've told a joke. You tell the joke and everybody laughs, and then you say, "But seriously, folks. . . ." That doesn't work. A joke has to tie in directly to the material that you're going to present, and you have to make that transition smoothly to make it effective. It's extremely difficult.

Yet another reason jokes are not successful openers

is that it is difficult to tell one well. You may tell jokes wonderfully in front of your family and friends, but that's completely different from telling it in front of a group, especially a group of strangers. If you're going to tell a joke of any kind, you need to practice it and practice it and practice it. Most professional speakers tell a joke or story forty or fifty times before they ever use it in a presentation.

Occasionally, jokes are appropriate to certain kinds of content; some jokes make fun of something or somebody in a way that might be appropriate for certain audiences. But there aren't too many, and they have to be used with extreme care. You may use them in the middle of your presentation, as support for a specific point, but never as an opener. I have been making professional presentations on all aspects of communications for over twenty years and there are three jokes that I tell, just three — and NONE is an opener. I am working on a fourth one, and after I spend more time telling it into tape recorders and to friends, I will use it in a speech. But it won't be an opener either. The bottom line is that jokes are risky and the risks usually outweigh the possible gain, especially when there are so many other excellent hooks.

WHAT ABOUT "GOOD MORNING"?

Resist in most situations the urge to begin with "Thank you," or "Good morning," or "I'm glad to be here" as the opener. There are several compelling reasons to avoid these old beginnings. First, they are old beginnings. These platitudes are so common that nobody listens to them, and you will not get the attention that you need from the audience. They will continue content-edly with their own thoughts until you rouse them. It is also difficult to deliver these old chestnuts with any degree of enthusiasm or excitement. In fact those who try enthusiasm on "Good morning" generally sound phony or foolish. Your opener must be an attention getter.

What about starting with your name? No built-in excitement there, I regret to tell you. It's a Catch-22: If you are a famous person the audience already knows you; if you aren't famous, your name won't get their rapt attention. Besides that, your name has generally been listed as speaker in the program; sometimes the intro-ducer gives your name: "Please help me welcome John Smith." (And yet haven't you heard some dim soul begin his talk following that exact introduction with "Hello, I'm John Smith"?)

If you feel compelled to utter those worn out words, you may certainly choose to do so at some point in your introduction — anyplace but the opener. For example, if the talk is to an environmental group, your introduction might begin this way: "We have one last chance to save this old growth forest! We have one last opportunity to preserve some of our heritage! We have one last chance to make a difference in the environment for our grand-children! . . . Good afternoon, I'm Jane Smith, and I'd like to tell you what we must do with this last opportunity."

POINTS TO REMEMBER

If you succeed in getting the rapt attention of the audience at the top of your talk, the rest will come more easily than you imagine.

The TO DO List:

Jot down opening lines that you can re-member; they may be openers that you have used, they may be ones you have heard. Decide to what extent were they successful in capturing the attention of the audience.

CHAPTER FOUR

INVOLVING THE AUDIENCE

The second goal of the introduction is to involve the members of the audience in your topic. The reason is simple: at the beginning they are listeners; your goal is to turn them into participants. You may have thought that presenting is you talking and the audience listening. However, even in a short talk you will have better success as a speaker if you involve the audience in some way. While involvement is an essential part of training or workshops, nearly all speaking to a group situations are enhanced when people feel as if they are participating rather than just observing.

Your ability to involve the audience and to get them to care about your topic will directly affect in a positive way your ability to reach your goal. If you remember that your ultimate goal is to get a specific message across, you will be eager to use fresh and original means of reaching that goal. By making people part of the process

—truly participants and not just observers or listeners—they are more attentive, they remember more, and they are more accepting of final ideas.

The degree of involvement you select is determined by time and by the type of presentation you give. Formal speeches generally require the least involvement, training sessions and meetings that you facilitate demand the most. Most talks will fall between those two extremes.

To begin the decision-making process of determining the degree of audience involvement desired, consider the needs, attitudes, and beliefs of this particular group based on your assessment of them in the communications triangle. Relate the involving aspect of your introduction to their concerns. In other words, speak from their need, not just from your own. If you have strong feelings about the topic, do tell them why. Clarify your position. Clarify your knowledge, your expertise, your experience, whatever it is that qualifies you to speak. Share a bit of yourself if you can, carefully, and pull the group toward you.

Beyond getting the audience to relate to you as a person, here are four primary methods of achieving involvement with your audiences:

- involve their minds
- involve them physically
- involve them in writing
- involve them orally.

DECISIONS ABOUT INVOLVEMENT ACTIVITIES

To decide what methods of involvement to use, ask yourself some questions: How much time do we have for involvement activities? How much involvement is needed to get a commitment from this audience? Will the audience be more willing participants if they are deeply involved?

INVOLVE THEIR MINDS

The quickest and simplest method to involve an audience in your presentation is to involve their minds; there are several ways to do that. Ask them a question, which they simply think about the answer to, or ask them to remember something or someone which is relevant to your topic. In customer service training, one of the involvers I like to use is to ask people to remember one place where they like to do business, shop, or to have a service done. Because I want to involve them in writing too, they jot down some specific reasons why they like this place of business. They quickly realize that they already know what good service means.

When you ask people to involve their minds in something related to your topic, you are getting them to move mentally from the arena where they are to the arena where you'd like them to be. And every presentation, no matter how short, can and should involve the audience at least mentally. Even in a twenty-minute breakfast talk, you should get them participating mentally in the topic that you are talking about.

INVOLVE THEM PHYSICALLY

The second method of involving the audience is to get them to do something physical. At the beginning of your presentation usually, you ask them to raise their

hands about something. What you're concerned about
here are preferences, demographics, background, experience. Several purposes are served. First, you involve the
audience physically when you ask them to raise their
hands. If they're sitting in their own little invisible iso-
lation boxes at the beginning of an early morning conference or a Saturday training session, they have not talked
to anyone, they are a little rigid or tense; getting them
to raise their hands not only involves their minds, it also
relaxes their bodies and makes them more receptive to
what you have to say.

There is another desirable and important outcome
of asking people to raise their hands about something:
As speaker, you find out additional information that you
need to know about demographics — how many of them
are homeowners, how long they have worked, how many
of them work for someone else, what their level of education or background is, how many of them own new
cars, how many of them come from out of state. . . . The
list is endless. And however much you have found out
about the audience ahead of time, there almost always
is something else that you'd like to find out or could find
out, which would help to individualize your talk. I recall
a story about a speaker who was to address a group of
taxi cab drivers. He made some assumptions about their
level of education and intelligence which he "forgot" to
validate with some questions at the beginning of his talk.
Unfortunately, the assumptions were far too low. Not only
was he unsuccessful in individualizing his talk, he was
unable to even complete it: He was booed off the stage.

Finally, asking people to demonstrate their background, their orientation, or their level of experience
helps the audience to understand its own diversity. If you
are covering a topic which is broad, some of the material
is apt to be basic, some likely to be more technical. Those
who are technical will wonder why you're boring them

with all of this background information. The people in the audience who are not technical will wonder why you're now speaking so technically. However, if you have asked people to raise their hands about how many years they have been working with computers, for example, then the audience will understand, "My, there's a big variety of people here. No wonder this speaker is covering so much." In other words, you help the audience to understand why you have chosen the material that you have by helping them to know who's present and what kinds of experience, backgrounds, and interests are involved. Look for applications for your own presentations.

INVOLVE THEM IN WRITING

A third method of involving the audience is to ask them to write. You can ask them to jot down three points, two aspects, five traits, or four features of something. Ask them to write down their expectations for the seminar or the training session. Ask them to write down the first three words that come to their minds when you mention the word "authority." Ask them to remember something or someone and write it down. In other words, involve people by getting them to translate thought into action through writing.

If you want to formalize the process, include a work sheet in your handouts so they can write these items down in a structured way. Another option is to put big pieces of butcher paper or newsprint on the wall. Ask people to list ideas, reactions, questions, problems, or concerns, on these sheets of paper around the room. This activity not only involves them in writing, it obviously gets them physically up to move around, and this can be a very helpful process. The goal in involving the audience is to get them to invest themselves in the importance of what you're talking about; any time you ask them to do something, you heighten the odds of success in achieving your purpose because they are more involved in the topic.

INVOLVE THEM ORALLY

Finally, you can involve people orally. This involvement approach is the very best one, even for some speech events, because at bottom most of us would rather talk than listen — especially if we can do so from the safety of a group.

Unless a speech is formal, you can involve people orally by using a socializing process. This is the minimal activity you can do orally, and it's an important one if you are going to ask people to participate. If you plan to ask them to share their feelings, or even to alter their feelings during the course of a presentation, socializing them first enhances your chances of success. If you are on a tight time schedule, this activity can be accomplished in as little as one minute. Ask them to turn to the persons on their left and right, introduce themselves and chat for a minute. This kind of involvement, quick as it is, minimizes the strangeness that people feel. They at least have some contact with someone else in the room, which makes them feel less isolated. (Socializing is less necessary, of course, if you are addressing an audience who know one another.)

For more oral involvement — for meetings, facilitation sessions, trainings — begin by doing any of the activities above, having people think, raise their hands, write, or speak. Then brainstorm ideas by having people repeat out loud to the group what they have to say. (With an audience that you sense will not be outgoing, you will get better responses if you follow this two-step process.) You may choose to write the ideas on a flip chart or a blackboard, or you can simply have them presented orally, depending on how much time you can invest or what other purposes the information may serve later.

A further way to involve people orally, if given sufficient time, is to ask them to break into pairs or small groups to discuss some specific aspect or question related to your subject. Complete that two-, five-, or ten-minute discussion with one of the follow-up options above. Sometimes it is enough to raise people's awareness that others have differing ideas, the same problems, or new insights and experiences. They are then more likely to be open to your suggestions and ideas.

Many variations of this activity exist. When there is time to go around the room, ask everyone to introduce herself, including, perhaps, something specific—what their goal for the session is, where they were born, one unusual aspect of their lives (having nothing to do with work, for example). Yet another variation is to follow the pairs activity by asking each to introduce the individual with whom he was paired.

The result of socializing a group prior to serious discussion is greater openness. Added bonuses of socializing activities are that 1) humorous information may come to light, and 2) people find strangers with whom they have something in common. Bonds are formed that improve the session.

If you engage in any oral involvement activity, be certain that you are able to regain control once the activity is complete. If you question your ability to call the group back to attentiveness, prepare a specific transition sentence which ties together what they have been doing with what you are going to do next.

As an extreme example of a need for audience

involvement, a client asked my advice on a particular training session she was to facilitate in which the audience was all managers and supervisors, peers of hers or higher. She had three strong concerns about the session: 1) controlling the group would be difficult, 2) certain individuals would likely dominate any discussions, and 3) the necessary discussion topics were apt to cause some heat and excitement.

My suggestion was to let the participants control each other. First, divide the audience into groups (using colored cards to predetermine the makeup of each group: reds together, blues together, etc.). Each group should be given one of the potentially heated topics to discuss fully. Then each group would present a summary of its comments and decisions, if any, to the entire group. This approach would help solve my client's concerns: everyone highly involved, timid people more apt to speak out in a smaller group, the trainer not having to "keep control" and — most significantly — during small group discussion extreme views would be sifted out. Reports from the small groups are likely to present consensus material. Discussion following the small group presentation allows other individuals to make extreme comments; however, the small group leaders will field those challenges, not the trainer.

POINTS TO REMEMBER

An audience whose status is changed from observers and listeners to participants is an audience which you can move further quicker in the direction you want them to go. If you have always just stood up and talked at people for the allotted amount of time, consider making a change: Share the time with your audience.

The TO DO List:

Begin a file of involving devices that you have experienced in training and talks you have given or heard. Keep adding to the file as you speak and as you hear others speak.

CHAPTER FIVE

DEVELOPING THE STRUCTURE

Content in a presentation of any type has two parts: the subject material and the structure that forms that material. Your central idea, the core of your message (as discussed in Chapter Two) is captured, refined, and expressed in your thesis sentence. That single sentence is the focus to which all other material in the speech is tested. Do these three points amplify the thesis? Does this example illustrate the thesis? Do these graphics elaborate upon or clarify the thesis? Your introduction must present that thesis (in all organizational plans but those which are totally inductive or indirect).

IDENTIFY YOUR CENTRAL IDEA—
THESIS SENTENCE

The third goal of the introduction is to identify your central idea. See page 44.

Through your opener, you lead your listeners to your general message; you then state your core idea, your thesis sentence. If you can also comfortably suggest your goal—to inform, to challenge, to educate—do so. But be subtle. As example, say "Zero-based budgeting is the solution to . . ." rather than, "I am going to convince you that zero-based budgeting is the solution to. . . ." Make sure there's no doubt of your thesis sentence.

The only exception to "include the thesis sentence" is a presentation in which your organizational plan is totally indirect: when you are presenting a highly controversial topic. In this case your only real chance of success is to use the inductive or indirect approach, developing your story first, building such a strong case that some of the audience—at least—will come around to your position by the time you state it at the climax of your presentation.

DEVELOP YOUR ORAL GUIDELINES

A final goal for an effective introduction is that it should name the major points of support. These points are the rest of the structure that the thesis sentence has introduced to the material. These major points become the oral guidelines. The oral guidelines are stated several times in your presentation: all together in the introduction to suggest the structure, individually as they provide ongoing structure, and usually in summary during the conclusion.

Oral guidelines have four purposes. They serve to

- force you to be prepared;
- name and number your major points of support;
- frame and divide the content;
- provide structure to help the audience follow your material.

First, oral guidelines force you, as the presenter, to be organized. They force you to know what your main items of support are going to be. They force you to have selected (from all the stuff you know about the subject) the 2% that's going to be particularly helpful and relevant for this particular audience. They force you to organize that 2% logically.

The oral guidelines name and number those major points of support that you have developed. The naming provides the framework that supports the presentation; the numbering divides the material logically no matter which organizational pattern you choose. Because your material is broken into smaller units of information, it is easier to absorb. This structure helps the audience to "see" the speech.

Finally, oral guidelines help the audience to help you succeed. They assist the audience in following your presentation and in listening effectively by enabling them to anticipate what you are going to say.

Consider the example of the minister who begins his sermon by saying, "The topic today is sin. There are three kinds of sin to examine this morning: your sin, my sin, and our sin." What the minister has done is not only name the guidelines, but also number them. The audience knows that there will be three different subtopics, three sections to the sermon. They are prepared to hear and absorb three points.

The minister gets into the body of his sermon by singly naming and numbering his first major point: "The first kind of sin for our attention this morning is **your** sin." He discusses, makes his comments, tells his relevant stories.

During the time that he's telling his support material, the audience tends to mentally drift away. People woolgather. They begin to think about other things. They notice the beautiful light coming in through the stained glass. They look at the wonderful flowers at the alter. The skillful minister knows this, so when he gets to the second main point, he not only repeats the oral guideline, he also repeats the number: "The second kind of sin is **my** sin." Delivery of oral guideline sentences needs to be handled carefully. (See Chapter Twelve.)

The minister then gives his support, the audience drifts away. How does he ever get them back? He gets them back with the oral guidelines—each time. The minister says, "And finally, ladies and gentlemen, we are forced to consider **our** sins." Once again he gathers up the audience and gets them all back listening.

Why does the audience need to be gathered? It's common knowledge that people can listen intently for no more than just a short while. If the speaker is extremely compelling, they may listen for a few minutes. No one listens intently for an entire ten minutes, fifteen minutes, especially an hour. That's why the oral guidelines are so important. They tell the audience how many main points there are going to be, and, as each main point occurs, they signal the audience that another key area is about to be presented.

People will listen as long as they need to, to get the point, to understand the concept; then their minds will drift away. You repeat the next oral guideline, numbering it carefully, "the third," "the fourth," "the final," so that they can tune in once again.

Remember when you were in school and your teacher said, "There will be four things on this test. Number one . . ." You took a note, but your mind drifted away and the next thing you heard was, "And the fourth thing . . ." You panicked. You leaned over to your neighbor and said, "Oh, wow! what are number two and number three?" What happened? The teacher probably neglected to number the second and third aspects as she mentioned them. If she had done so accurately and appropriately, you would probably have tuned back in.

These are oral guidelines. They are names and numbers which are important for you in organizing. They are equally important for your audience in helping you to succeed by anticipating what you're going to say and by tuning in to listen as you develop each of your major supporting points. The same speech can be given, with the same support and examples, but without oral guidelines; that is, one uninterrupted long speech. However, the oral guidelines turn one long speech into several shorter more graspable sections, each of which can be absorbed individually. Don't miss the chance to help your audience help you to succeed. Provide the listening structure of oral guidelines.

PATTERNS FOR INTRODUCTIONS

As you can see, introductions have primary parts including the opener, an involver, the thesis sentence and the oral guidelines. Here are five different patterns that introductions may take.

A **direct approach**, where you state the thesis first, add an involver, then provide the oral guidelines. In that case, of course, your thesis will be your opener.

An **indirect approach**, in which you have an opener, then your oral guidelines, and finally your thesis sentence.

A **V-shaped introduction**, which begins with a general statement about your subject and narrows logically through several succeeding sentences down to your thesis. Then your oral guidelines will be named.

An **I-shaped introduction** is one which has a general statement of purpose as the opener, perhaps some involvement activity, then your oral guidelines. The introduction closes with a restatement of your purpose as the thesis sentence in a more specific and emphatic way.

An **inverted T-shape** begins with a tight series of logical points and is followed by your thesis sentence. The oral guidelines may be a part of the logical points or may follow the thesis.

POINTS TO REMEMBER

Structure helps you organize and focus; it helps your audience anticipate you and follow you. Structure will thus help you succeed.

CHAPTER SIX

DEVELOPING THE CONTENT

If you have assessed the triangle and planned as has been suggested up to this point, developing the content is an easy process, whether you create an extemporaneous presentation for note cards or write a manuscript. First, return to the triangle to make sure that you are comfortable with the decisions that you have made and the notes you've taken. Reconfirm your purpose — to get action, to persuade or convince, to build goodwill, to teach, to train. Write your final thesis sentence if you have not done so. If it is already written, reassess it, tighten it up, adjust its focus. Remember the Two Percent Rule, to support that thesis with the appropriate 2% of what you know. And, if you haven't done so, create the oral guidelines.

DECIDE ON MATERIAL
TO SUPPORT THE STRUCTURE

Remember that content has two parts: structure and material. Your oral guidelines (Chapter Five) have developed the structure. Your last phase is to develop the material to support the structure.

Think about the 2%. If you try to say all you know or much of what you know, your presentation turns out to be heavy, dense with ideas, facts, and information. That's not only hard to listen to, it's difficult to remember. The goal is two or three points which are amplified, supported, supplemented, and expanded. Use interesting anecdotes, illustrations, experiences, stories from your experience. If you think about presentations that you have heard, what you are most likely to remember is the wonderful story that the speaker told to illustrate the point he was making. Isn't it counterproductive if what people remember is the story that illustrates the point rather than the point itself? Not if the story makes the point.

Your content may also be explanations, descriptions, examples, statistics, past experiences — material that you can make come alive for your audience. Much of this support material may also be created visually. (See Chapter Eight for information.)

By forcing yourself to develop and support only two or three oral guidelines, you are requiring yourself to create a content that will be interesting and relevant and meaningful to this particular audience.

NOTE CARDS

After you have created your presentation, prior to practicing it, you will want to put it on some note cards. Put the introduction and the conclusion on cards of different colors; use white for all the others. Use three-by-five cards or four-by-six cards but no larger. Why? Use cards because they are stiff enough to not rattle or fold up. Use small cards because if you use larger cards, you will be tempted to write out too much.

The first card should be a colored card, and it should have written out word for word your opener and your thesis sentence. The oral guidelines should be numbered on the second card, which is white. Put one or two points and sub-points on each card. Be sure that you do not have an entire deck by the time you finish. Your conclusion should also be written out completely, on a card of a different color.

The reason for the color coding is simple. You want to be able to identify the first card and the last card without having to pause to look carefully. Speakers typically use the cards early in the presentation, but do not refer to them much as the speech goes on. After you've been speaking for several minutes and are ready to conclude, you want the exact conclusion sentence that you crafted beautifully. If the card is colored, with your peripheral vision you can locate it in the deck and easily move it to the top. However, if your conclusion is not on a colored card, you will have to laboriously stop and search through the cards that you have not used in order to find the final one. That pause sabotages your momentum and leaves you feeling a little hesitant and uncertain, sometimes even embarrassed.

MANUSCRIPT PRESENTATIONS

If you are presenting to a group where your information must be exact or precise, you may decide that your best recourse is a manuscript presentation. A manuscript presentation is exact words, exact sentences. You deliver it rather than read it; write the material for the ear, not the eye. The easiest way to capture the sound of "talk" is to speak your presentation from an outline into a tape recorder. Transcribe it; use the transcription as the basis for writing the draft of the actual manuscript. Continue speaking it out loud, refining phrases and altering words, until it sounds like talk—your talk.

The words you choose for the manuscript need to be words from your speaking vocabulary, not your writing vocabulary and certainly not from your reading vocabulary. Most of us understand many words in reading from context that we barely know; when we write we tend too often to use words that we don't use in everyday conversation. The manuscript (in most instances) should be composed of only the words in our smallest vocabulary, the speaking one. In other words, if you wouldn't use a word in talking face to face with someone, it doesn't belong in your manuscript presentation either.

If someone is writing the speech for you, be certain that you give them as much input as you can during their drafting process. Once it's in draft form, follow the same steps to achieve a conversational tone and style that sound like you.

Re-create it on the paper so that it is easily delivered. The text needs to be typed or printed triple-spaced with the largest type that you can reasonably use. Use a regular mix of capital letters and lower case so that you can scan it rather than having to look at every single letter. After you have created it in this large, widely-spaced type, practice delivering it.

First, you will need to mark it for delivery. Before you mark it, read the presentation out loud several times experimenting with the emphasis and the pacing, perhaps marking with a pencil. The third or fourth time that you go through it, you will sense yourself beginning to know about the pausing, the phrasing, the emphasis. Then you can use your colored felt pens to annotate the presentation material. Use different colored felt pens to mark long pauses, emphasis, changes in pitch, tone, and speed. You may decide, for example, to have red be pauses, blue be emphasis, yellow be slow down. Naturally, you don't want your coding to be too complicated or it will defeat its purpose. You must practice it enough after it is annotated that the material can lie flat on the podium, and you can establish frequent and extensive eye contact with the audience. They will be able to tell that you are doing a manuscript. That's not a problem. Your goal is to deliver it in such a way that it is still memorable and dynamic.

WAYS TO EMPHASIZE AN IDEA

Emphasizing important material is another aspect of presenting that includes both development and delivery. Your audience takes its cue from you about how important an idea, a concept, a thought, a word, a phrase is. There are many ways that you can emphasize an idea. Some methods are verbal, some are visual, and some are non-verbal. These seven are particularly significant:

1. **Say it is important**. Use the word "key," "vital," "significant," "important." Let people know that in your

estimation as expert presenter, as speaker, that this is important by labeling it as such.

2. **Number it** as with oral guidelines: "the first consideration," "the second consideration." Perhaps even in subheadings: "the first point," "the second point," "the third point."

3. **Use your voice**. Use the instrument that you have to deliver. Make the idea louder. Put greater intonation on your word. Inflect the word in a different way. Slow down your voice speed so that your voice is indicating here's a different piece. The reason that this will help to emphasize is that any time you change your pitch or speed the audience is going to pay additional attention.

4. **Use a gesture**. Sweep your hand up in a grand motion. Pound your fist. Make a fist and wave it in the air. Make a circle to include everyone.

5. **Use pauses**. Pauses are verbal white space and they create attention on an idea in the same way that white space around something in an advertisement creates attention. Before you say it, pause a long time so that people who are listening to the sound of your voice rather than listening to your words will get an interruption in their mental wandering and will tune you in again. Pause after you say it to allow it to sink in, to allow people to absorb it.

6. **Repeat it**. Anything that is particularly important not only can be repeated, but should be repeated so that people have a chance to absorb it. When you consider, as we have done, how ineffectively people listen, you recognize that you owe it to an important idea to employ one or two or three or any number of these seven methods of emphasizing an idea.

7. **Reinforce it with a visual**. If it is true that we learn best by hearing, seeing, and doing, you can accomplish at least the first two. (In a long presentation or a training session you can accomplish all three, in fact.)

CLOSINGS

After you have finished presenting the body of your presentation, your oral guidelines, and the support material for those guidelines, you come at last to the finish. This is the closing. In terms of structure and organization, think of the closing as a paragraph in the same way that you think of the introduction as a paragraph. There are four features of a closing:

- Signal that the finish is near.
- Restate your thesis or key point.
- Summarize the main sub-points or oral guidelines.
- Have a finished tone in your voice and in your body language.

Though there are two aspects in a presentation, the content and the delivery, it is impossible in most instances to separate the two. The closing is certainly that way; your development of the closing should be closely tied to how you are going to deliver it.

In the best of all possible worlds, the speaker is able to let the audience know that she is coming to the close with her body, with her voice, and with the way she handles the ending of the last oral guideline. However, in the real world, most of us need to signal that the end is arriving. This signal is much like an oral guideline. It is designed to remind the audience to tune back in for the last message. Some speech trainers and teachers say that it is inappropriate to say, "In summary" or "In conclusion" or "To close"; however, it is better to use a verbal signal of that sort than for the audience not to know that you are presenting your concluding remarks.

Your goal when you come to the finish is to gear

up for the final charge. At some point in the conclusion you will restate your thesis sentence. A sophisticated speaker may have a different way of phrasing the thesis sentence, but she needn't, and you don't need to either. If that sentence is the carefully crafted essence of the message that you wish to communicate, you will be perfectly appropriate if you repeat it word for word as a part of the conclusion, even though you've already used it in the introduction. This sentence is, after all, the heart of your message.

The other pieces of information that you want to remind the audience of are the main points (the oral guidelines), if your presentation is long enough that such reinforcement will be appropriate. How long is long enough? You'll have to be the judge of that. If you are giving a five- or ten-minute presentation, you might not wish to repeat the main points. However, in direct proportion to how significant the main points are in helping understand the thesis, you will wish to restate them in some form.

Whether you repeat the thesis sentence first and follow with the summary of the main points, or whether you summarize first and finish up with your thesis is something you will have to decide. Here are examples of each approach:

Thesis first—
"Today is our last chance to protect these wetlands. They provide jobs, promote a full complement of waterfowl and animal life, and enhance all our lives. Do your part!"

Thesis last—
"These wetlands provide jobs, promote a full complement of waterfowl and animal life, and enhance all

our lives. Today is our last chance to protect these valuable wetlands!"

The fourth feature of closings is a finished tone in the delivery aspects of your voice and body. A finished tone means a measured pace, a firm emphatic voice, a dramatic tone. You want the way you speak the sentences in your closing to reflect the importance that the words have; the delivery will be more deliberate than the delivery of the content. Say those sentences with particular emphasis on the key words. Deliver them in such a way that they have the significance that you want the audience to recognize.

The same will be true of your gestures. Your goal is to wind up on a high note. Be sure that you are putting forth your very best delivery. These are the sentences that the audience will have ringing in its ears as you finish. (More about delivery in Chapter Twelve.)

POINTS TO REMEMBER

1. Two percent of your knowledge, expanded with interesting information to fill the time of the speech, is more fun to listen to—and usually more successful —than a speech which tries to convey too much information.
2. The audience knows what's important by your signals.
3. Signal your closing and then hit it hard.
4. Leave no doubt in the minds of your audience what your message is.

CHAPTER SEVEN

PLANNING TEAM PRESENTATIONS

Many people present as part of a team to an audience of a few or a great number. Sales presentations and proposals are often handled by a team of two or more people. Your team presentation must reflect the same quality of teamwork that your firm's work demonstrates. Many sales have been lost because the team presentation was so unorganized, so slapdash, so contradictory, that the prospective client found it difficult to believe that the company could work in a unified way to service the account. I vividly remember an anguished call, some years ago, from a client who had fallen victim to this exact problem. Their three-year commitment to provide a service to a large municipal government was up for re-bid. Being confident because of their incumbent status, they did not bother to prepare much for the proposal, and they did not call me to help them prepare a dry run.

The result you can anticipate: they lost the bid.

When they inquired why they lost, they were told that their presentation had been so poorly organized that the municipality doubted whether the firm could work successfully as a team to complete the terms of another three-year contract.

The key for success in team presentations is a leader in charge of a smooth unit. A designated leader is essential, first of all, simply because someone has to make the thing move along. Someone has to be responsible for making sure that the presentation is ready to go, that the team is functioning smoothly.

There are four essentials for successful team presentations: Planning, Presentation, Follow-up, and Debriefing.

PLANNING

Successful pre-presentation planning includes these aspects:

- Participants and their roles
- Agenda
- Environment
- Equipment
- Time
- Briefing.

▪ PARTICIPANTS AND THEIR ROLES

The first decision that needs to be made about a team presentation is who the participants will be. Sometimes that's easy, other times it is not so easy. Depending on the importance and size of the client or audience, and on logistics, there may be several people who could participate. Someone needs to make the decision about who is going to fulfill which roles.

These questions need to be asked as the team is decided upon: Who is participating? What is each participant going to say? How long does each presenter have to speak? When during the presentation is each person going to present? As simple as those questions seem to be, the downfall of many team presentations comes right here: the decisions of separation of subject matter were not clearly made, people were not prepared to talk about certain aspects with authority and credibility. The team broke down at this simple first part.

▪ AGENDA

The agenda can take many forms. The leader or the group doing the planning will decide whether the agenda should be 1) written and presented ahead of time, 2) written and presented at the beginning of the meeting, 3) presented orally at the beginning of the meeting, 4) informally written on the board (a dry erase board, a flip chart, a blackboard). The choice essentially dictates (or is dictated by) what degree of formality you wish the presentation to reflect. To have the agenda written and distributed ahead of time is the most formal, with the least formal being a handwritten agenda on the board prior to the beginning of the meeting.

Why is an agenda of some kind important? First, it helps allocate and control time. It's easy for time to get away from people. It's easy for some presenters to talk too long. It's easy for the question and answer session to go on too long. It's easy, if you have questions answered during the presentation, for one section to dominate. The agenda empowers the leader to get the session back on track. The agenda empowers the leader to be able to say, "We'd like to spend some more time answering these questions after the session, but perhaps we ought to move on to Section Two."

A second purpose of the agenda is to define the tasks and specify the objectives of the presentation. The agenda indicates the flow of ideas in the material, sets the order of the participants. The agenda, like the oral guidelines, enables the audience to help you to succeed because it helps them to anticipate what's going to happen. An agenda also indicates time and position for the sub-events, such as visual presentations, films, video clips. It can outline housekeeping details such as whether questions will be taken at the end of each section, or if there will be a separate question and answer session. The agenda ensures that you are prepared. It helps the audience to anticipate you, and it imposes a degree of formality and organization onto the presentation which helps it to be smooth and contributes to the appearance of a smooth-running team.

▪ ENVIRONMENT

Another part of physical structuring and environment involves whether the meeting should be at your location, at the prospective client's or audience's location, or at a neutral site. There are some subtle, but important, psychological aspects here which are worth considering when you have a choice.

On your site you have more control. At the client's site he has more control. Your own turf gives you more authority. A neutral site encourages more openness, allows for greater equality of contact between the audience and the presenter.

Wherever you meet, to the extent that you are able, create an environment that reflects the kind of presentation that you want, the kind of interaction that you're looking for. The right environment gives you the best opportunity to have the authority and impact that you want.

You need to decide on the physical structure of the meeting room. Be sure you have the right size and shape room and the right configuration of chairs or tables for the type of meeting you are going to give. A semicircle or a U-shaped arrangement will encourage equal participation or equal feeling, even though your team is going to be presenting at the front. These setups allow everyone to have good eye contact, but allow the leader and the team to stand, to be in the position of control. (See Chapter Nine for further details about room setups.)

In most situations the speaker should stand to present. (see page 27.) It is important that the team members not speaking be seated so they can look at the audience in order to monitor audience reaction. In some situations the speaker is at the front of the table and the team members are right beside the spokesperson. They are doing what they think is appropriate: looking at the speaker, not at the audience. The result is they will not be able to see the faces in the audience. At least one member of the team needs to be able to see everybody in the audience so that he can watch their facial expressions and make appropriate notes about what aspects get reactions that will need further discussion.

▪ EQUIPMENT

If there are going to be visual aids, somebody has to be responsible for making sure that the appropriate equipment is available and that it works. That someone should be the leader. (Chapter Nine covers arranging for and handling audio-visual equipment.)

▪ TIME

Certain times of the day are better for presenting than others. I think everyone who's ever presented or lectured recognizes that the first thing on Saturday morning requires tremendous dynamic delivery. Right after lunch on a warm, sunny afternoon requires lots of audience involvement, some physical activity to make sure that people are going to be able to overcome the torpor that they feel after lunch. Last thing in the afternoon, just before the cocktail party, is a very difficult time to present. The audience is looking forward to its next activity more than it is looking forward to your presentation.

What does all this mean to you? If you have a chance to select the time or to have input about the time of your presentation, think about those considerations.

▪ BRIEFING

A team of presenters can be smooth only by being prepared. Planning makes the preparation work for the team while each individual can be responsible for his own piece of the program. However, a dry run is extremely important for creating a team which looks as if it works beautifully together. Review who's doing what when, how aspects are going to be phrased, what consistency there will be in terms of language, tone, and approach. Do not wing it unless the circumstances absolutely preclude a briefing session or practice. Invest a few minutes to gain greater efficiency, greater poise, and a sale—or a positive feeling from your staff or your special interest group.

PRESENTING

The presentation will be made by the spokesperson and each participant in turn. It is the spokesperson's responsibility, whether she is the leader or a person designated by the leader, to identify herself to the audience. As the presentation begins it is important to know who is in charge.

In addition to handling the introductions and the close of the overall presentation (and whatever participation the spokesperson is going to have during the presentation), the spokesperson has two other functions: One is to introduce the program and the people; the second is to be in charge of transitions.

The introduction to the program includes the presentation of the agenda (in whatever manner it's going to be presented), the statement of the oral guidelines (in much the same way that part of the introduction is handled in an individual speech), and any house rules that are apt to be important (such as, "Please jot down your questions and we'll have a question and answer session at the end of the presentation").

The spokesperson sometimes handles the introduction of the team and the presentation of their background. However, this phase can be handled in different ways depending on the amount of time that's available. The most efficient way is for the spokesperson to introduce each team member, giving their credentials at the same time. Though efficient, that's not as satisfactory as having all team members give their own names and briefly state their own credentials, for a couple of reasons. The audience gets a chance to have some contact with each of these team presenters at the beginning. That's good for the audience. Speaking one's own name and credentials helps the team members begin to relax. Once your voice has been activated and you have made a comment or two, you start to relieve any nervousness and anxiety (as we will discuss in Chapters Ten and Twelve.)

It is important, if people are to introduce themselves, that each person has her background tightly described and presented in just a sentence or two. Half of your presentation time can pass while a verbose team member is going on too long.

In most team presentation situations each presenter should think about his portion as a small, complete speech; that is, it has potential to stand alone. Even though an individual piece of the team presentation — on the benefits of this particular product for the prospective client, for example — is only five minutes long, it needs to have a good opener, good oral guidelines, and a good close. Each piece of the team presentation should thus be a mini-presentation; these mini-presentations, able to stand alone individually, add up to a strong overall presentation.

The second major role of the spokesperson is to be in charge of transitions. This passing of the baton from one player to the next is the second area where teams break down. This breakdown need not occur. The transitions may be verbal. The transitions may be as simple as a non-verbal gesture to the next individual. However they are handled, they must be smooth, consistent, and carefully thought out so that the audience perceives once again a smoothly running unit. For example, if each person is to introduce the next presenter, she will first finish her section with a strong conclusion statement; next a significant pause, to let that statement sink in; and finally, she will offer a small gesture and say, "Jack Smith will give you the marketing perspective." If the spokesperson is to make the transition statement, she will wait for that same significant pause, and make the same introductory statement. If members are introducing themselves, the person who is next will wait for that same pause, then begin, "I'm Jack Smith. The marketing perspective on the project is. . . ." The strong pause before the transition is the key at all times.

As each person is speaking, all the other team members have a specific role to be playing. That role is to monitor the verbal and non-verbal reactions of the audience, especially of the decision-makers in the audience. The non-speakers need to take specific notes about aspects that got strong reaction—positive, negative, curiosity, confusion—all of those qualities that are possible to see on a person's face and in a person's non-verbal communications. Those are the aspects that need clarification or that someone in the audience appears to need to know more about. One of the advantages of being a team is having someone to monitor reactions and add comments when something has not been presented fully or accurately.

At the end of each person's section, that person may say (or perhaps the spokesperson would say), looking at the rest of the panel, "Would you like to add anything?" If you were monitoring non-verbal behavior and you noticed that one particular point about finances caused some raised eyebrows, you would nod and say, "Let me just add that the quality of the material is directly related to its price and we have made an effort to find the finest quality of material because we want this piece of equipment to last a long time." Or when the person who has just finished speaking says, "Like to add anything?" you may say, "Let me just add that . . ." or "I might just make a note that . . ." or "It might be helpful to remind us that. . . ." In other words, use a positive sentence which contributes a little extra piece of information that you think will be helpful.

What about interruptions? In terms of the physical aspects of adding these comments, first of all, try not to interrupt a speaker. I have seen presentations in which the presenter went on at much too great a length because the team had not practiced. Or the presenter was using the wrong level of language. Perhaps he was talking very technically, and the audience was not technical; or she was talking dollars too early in the presentation; or he got sidetracked in a way that was seriously detrimental to the presentation. In those kinds of situations it is crucial to politely interrupt, in order to get the presentation back on track. There's no point in sitting there seeing your entire team sunk to the bottom by one presenter who is not prepared or not appropriate. Naturally, this must be handled with great care. Clearly, it's best if the spokesperson does the tactful interruption to re-structure the presentation; but if the spokesperson does not, then another member of the team perhaps should do it. You try to find a spot where the speaker has stopped for breath, and you say with as much warmth and positiveness as you can, "Sam, if I might just interrupt here for a moment . . ." and make your rectifying comment.

Interruptions are only for crucial situations. Interruptions can indicate some disharmony, but if they're handled well, it's much better to have a little disharmony than to have the entire presentation ruined because there was a crucial problem left uncorrected. The audience won't remember the interruption; they **will** remember the unsuccessful presentation.

As a group, you will have decided earlier how questions are to be handled, and the leader will have announced this decision as a part of housekeeping comments. Allowing questions following each section is generally preferable, because it involves the audience throughout the presentation. The leader should be certain that he can smoothly get the Q & A started. (Consult Chapter Sixteen.) To provide poised, credible responses, use the tips for handling difficult questions in Chapter Seventeen; make certain that all team members know how to **appropriately** re-direct a question (see page 199).

The spokesperson generally also handles the close. The entire presentation needs a strong conclusion just as a solo speech does. If you are selling, ask for the order. If you are seeking financial assistance for an environmental project, ask for the money. If it's staff morale you seek to boost, close with, "We can do it. We need your help!"

FOLLOW-UP

Sometimes arrangements about the follow-up are handled near the end of the presentation; sometimes the follow-up discussion is handled after the formal presentation is finished. Which approach you use will be decided, of course, in the briefing as part of the planning process. And it's also important to know who's going to do that. Is the spokesperson going to make the follow-up statement or comment, or is there another individual on the team who is going to handle that detail?

DEBRIEFING

Unless you are never, ever, going to present as a team again, it's vital to have a debriefing session. There are two areas, of course, to be discussed: What did we do well? What could we do better next time? It's important, especially if the team is composed of some senior staff and some junior staff, some executives and some support staff, that this be an arena of equality. Each participant should be encouraged to feel equally free to make comments, both about good things and about things that need to be improved. In addition to improving the efforts of the team, this is an opportunity for professional growth, not a criticism experience. But honesty is crucial.

The reason that it's important to start with "What did we do well?" is that you want to build on feelings of satisfaction. Each presenter has a chance to get a compliment, a chance to give a compliment to someone else, and a chance to reinforce for the team the aspects that were successful. Even more important is the "What should we do better next time?" because the team must grow from each team presentation in the same way that as an individual presenter you wish to grow. Because there were several of you present, you each have a unique opportunity to get instant feedback from people who were actually there listening and watching.

The debriefing should take place as soon after the presentation as possible. If you are separating and not able to debrief immediately, it is an excellent idea for each presenter to take a few notes as soon as possible after the session while the thoughts are fresh, so the aspects that need to be improved can be discussed in the most productive way later.

Phrase those comments with positive language. Instead of saying, "You didn't . . ." try to say, "Next time, why don't you try. . . ." Sometimes the non-presenters sit and look solemn for instance, and there's a temptation in the debrief to say, "You didn't smile. You looked so glum sitting there." And, of course, that's a criticism. It's difficult for most of us to accept criticism. Much better to say, "In the next team presentation, it would be wonderful if everybody on the team could look more enthusiastic and have smiles on their faces and look more actively involved in the process." That kind of positive language gives people something to grow toward, something that they can do differently, whereas a criticism is simply a slap across the side of the head.

POINTS TO REMEMBER

Planning is essential. Practice is important. The key to team unity and effectiveness is a leader who has made sure that everything will be smooth.

The TO DO List:

Critique the last team presentation that you participated in; include thoughts about the overall success, your performance, the performance of others. It is never too late to debrief the presentation, in order to improve the next one.

CHAPTER EIGHT

PREPARING EFFECTIVE VISUALS

Visual aids are supposed to do exactly what they say: aid you in the successful presentation of your message. You are the speaker, delivering a message. Visual aids support your verbal efforts; they do not replace your words and they should not overwhelm your words. Those speakers who hide behind a session which flashes 80 slides in 60 minutes at an unsuspecting audience have not yet learned that basic lesson.

WHY VISUALS?

Visuals are vital for success in the public speaking world today, however, for two key reasons, both related to technology. The first reason is that an increasing number of members in your audiences have grown up with television. They are accustomed to, one might even go so far as to say they demand, color, flash and glitter. Television viewers are used to high profile excitement when being pitched. Few visual aids can replicate television (although videotaped segments attempt to, if the budget is available). Yet the speaker who attempts to win an audience to her point without visuals must be a superb speaker with a compelling message and spellbinding delivery. Most of us speakers are not (yet) spellbinders.

The second reason that creating visual aids is important today is that technology has made it relatively easy to create them. Computer programs which create graphics abound; many programs draw and paint; large size type, fancy fonts, and attractive borders are all available at the press of a key. Entrepreneurs have set up shops whose sole purpose is turning your rough sketch into a drawing, an elegant layout, or a great word slide. In fact, you can be looked upon as a trifle lazy or at least out of touch with the rest of the world if you do not have visuals. Your audience is apt to wonder where you have been the last decade.

Are there times when no visuals should be used? Yes: when you do not have the budget to create visuals which are equal in quality to the work, service, or cause about which you are speaking. Visuals reflect upon your image in the same way that your appearance does, (in fact, in the same way that your professional brochure and business card do). If second-rate visuals will adversely affect your image, avoid them. Develop and use your vocal instrument to its fullest.

As a professional you should be well aware of the kinds of graphics that are used in your profession. You became familiar with them while developing your professional tools and reading technical journals or periodicals. Certain kinds of materials — and thus certain professions — lend themselves to specific types of graphics and other visuals. If you are making a presentation to a group other than your peers, you should read professional magazines associated with that particular audience to find out what kind of visuals they relate to best. As with your content, visuals should evolve from the perspective of the audience, not from your perspective.

WHAT VISUALS?

Effective visual aids capture many words in a single picture, diagram, or phrase. Clarity and simplicity are the goals. Turn concepts into evocative pictures, numbers into dramatic graphs, complex systems into simple flow charts. Sometimes there is an effective visual sitting around your work place: scientists have intriguing apparatus; architects have cunning scale models; foresters have tiny seedlings. Most every profession has a variety of colorful posters which can be used with success. Just because an item is commonplace to you, do not overlook its potential as an exciting or meaningful visual for an audience. "Found objects," or props, which represent a metaphor or simile for your audience can heighten interest.

The most dramatic visual I have ever seen was brought to a civic group by a chiropractor: she strode up to the front of the room carrying a three-foot model of a curved object with lots of segments and uneven edges. She began her presentation with a question in a compelling voice, "How many of you have one of these?" Few hands were raised. "You **all** do. . . . It's a **spine**," she said, and we all laughed. Then she walked silently around the room allowing us to touch it, run our fingers over the nerve nodules and get "up close and personal" with an object that we are all familiar with in other contexts. It was a fantastic opener, a wonderful visual aid, and a successful presentation.

If you are in business, most of your visuals are apt to be graphics. Graphics can be classified into four basic categories, depending on the material they are to represent: for numbers, for systems, for physical items, and for people.

GRAPHICS FOR NUMBERS, STATISTICS, AND FINANCIAL DATA

Your goal here is to translate numbers—dollars, percents, degrees, or demographics—into pictures, for clarity, for simplicity, and for emphasis. The graphic devices you use may include bar charts, pie charts, graphs, and pictographs. Do be aware that popular newspapers and business magazines have gone too far with cute pictographs and clever frames for their bar charts and pie charts. Too far, that is, for a business presentation. If you are presenting informally, your only concern with clever backgrounds and frames is whether they distract from the point your visual is making.

Avoid tables. Though the use of tables is common, they are not acceptable as visual aids. The numbers are too small to be read beyond the third row. I had a client who had asked for speech delivery advice but had not asked for advice about visuals. As I videotaped his presentation I was forced to witness the worst case of "ineffective table-itis" I had ever seen. The speaker was a noted management consultant; his audience, a group of accountants. The first full-page table appeared, accompanied by these words, "I know you can't see the numbers in this table. I wish you could because the numbers tell the story."

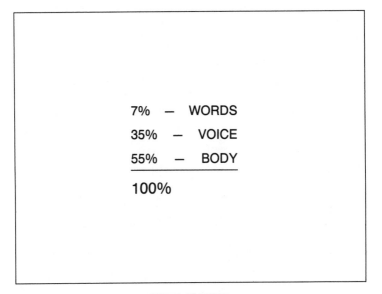

POOR VISUAL

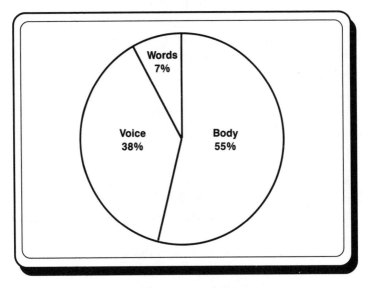

IMPROVED VERSION

Everyone has heard speakers say that they know the audience can't see their tables. If they know we can't see them, why are they using them?

Tables are also too complex; they contain data that is irrelevant to the point. One of my sophisticated financial clients tended to just try to get by with a transparency of whatever page from their proposal that they thought had good information on it. This approach was easy, but almost totally unsuccessful, for three reasons: the visuals depicted a more complex story than the speaker wanted to convey at that point; the numbers were too tiny to be read by most of the audience; the visuals were busy.

Busy transparencies are a problem almost anytime a speaker tries to simply copy the page of a proposal or report onto a blank sheet. The transparency typically has not only the numbers or charts, but also the firm name, the client name, the name of the proposal, the framework around the chart and the page number of the report.

It is easy to physically cut out the chart or graph, enlarge it on the copier and then run it through on a transparency. The extraneous matter will be left behind and the graphic will be large enough to be viewed. (See pages 110 and 111.)

For financial data, translate the significant data into a simple chart or graph which speaks for itself.

GRAPHICS FOR SYSTEMS, ORGANIZATION, FLOW, AND TIME LINES

Your goal here is to show motion, systematic development, relationships, steps, order, or to simplify systems and concepts. It takes many words to verbally describe what is simple to illustrate graphically. Imagine how many words it would take to explain the typical organizational tree: what the layers of management are, which divisions report to which senior managers, which departments come under which division. It would never stop! Your choices in this category include organizational charts, trees, flow charts, Warnier-Orr diagrams and Gantt charts.

GRAPHICS FOR PHYSICAL ITEMS

The category of graphics available for depicting physical items is designed to show the relationship of parts to a whole, to illustrate physical systems, to clarify intricate design and development, to show physical connections, to demonstrate complexity. Professions which use such aids would not function day to day without them. Yet too few speakers from these professions take the extra time needed to create speech visuals which could give greater life and vigor to their presentations. Graphics in this category include drawings, exploded drawings, cutaway drawings, renderings, photographs, diagrams, and maps.

When reproducing a picture of a physical item for a visual, be careful to limit the amount of information that you plan to show. The biggest error is making the reproduction too complex; the second serious error is labeling all the parts and/or fields. While perhaps logical that precise professionals in engineering, software development, or science wish to include all the details (just as financial types want to include the complete "picture" with all the numbers), they do so at their peril. The audience needs simple uncluttered visuals to observe and learn from. Once again, prepare what the audience needs and can understand, not what you would like to offer.

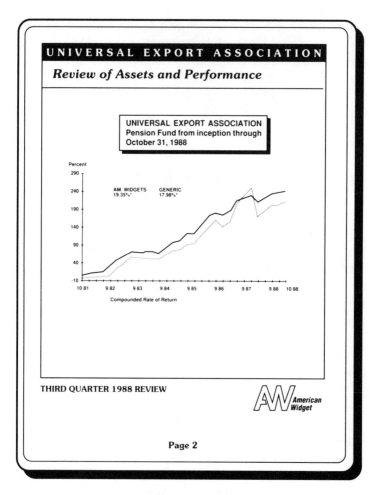

POOR GRAPHIC

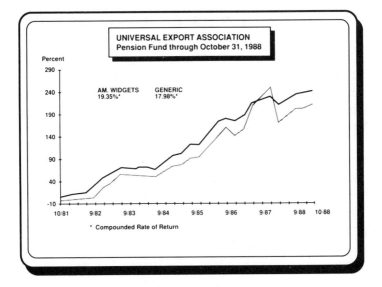

IMPROVED VERSION

A software company preparing for a national two-day marketing and training seminar asked my advice for polishing their presenters. As one speaker after another was unable to stay even close to his allotted time, it became evident that the problem rested in the visuals. Because each diagram contained too much detail, the speakers found themselves explaining every one of those details, rather than just the ones they had prepared to cover. When we whited out some of the detail the speakers returned to their prepared notes and finished on time.

GRAPHICS FOR PEOPLE SITUATIONS

The fourth category of graphics to develop for presentations is people situations. You may be creating safety reminders, physical training, new production procedures. Choices include sketches, cartoons, and line drawings. Use humor and exaggeration in any way that you can.

Notice that there is no category here called "word visuals." Does that mean that word visuals are not acceptable? It does not mean that. It does mean that you should develop word visuals only as a last resort. Words are not "visual." Word visuals (especially for overhead transparencies and slides) are easiest to create; unfortunately so, because they are also the most boring and least successful. If you begin, out of habit, to create word visuals, challenge yourself to translate some of them into more interesting graphics.

Material for some professions, however, lends itself to word visuals. If yours is one of those, follow the guidelines below especially carefully.

GUIDELINES FOR BETTER VISUALS

1. Aim for cleanness and clarity. Resist the impulse to be too fancy; even though your computer system enables you to mix six different type faces, don't. Don't let the art overwhelm the message.

2. Aim for simplicity. When using a drawing of a mechanism, for example, resist the temptation to fill in or label all the fields or parts. Include enough detail for authenticity. Label those parts necessary to make the point that that specific graphic is supporting, plus one or two major items for perspective.

3. When developing word visuals, be brief. Use words or short phrases, not sentences. Use single-syllable words whenever possible. Use common abbreviations (you can explain them as you debrief the slide).

4. Use capitals and lower case lettering rather than all caps. People read more quickly by scanning the ascenders and descenders (the parts of letters which come above and below the regular line of type). Use bold when you want extra emphasis, instead of capital letters.

5. Use color. Remember what your audience sees on television. But resist the opportunity to be gaudy.

6. Headings or titles should usually be in large type. Subheads should be in the same font (type style), with smaller type than the headings. Consider bold or some other special treatment for emphasis of a key word or phrase.

7. For bold visual impact on short lists, use bullets, closed boxes, or closed circles rather than asterisks or open characters.

8. If you have more than three items in a subhead consider numbering or lettering them. If the items must be taken in order—they are steps in a process for example —it is important to number them. You remind the audience of the importance of keeping them in order.

NOTE—if the material requires more depth than subheads, print that extra material only on the paper copy of the handouts that you give the audience. (See page 170.) An overhead or slide should generally have only the title and the briefly phrased, bulleted subheads.

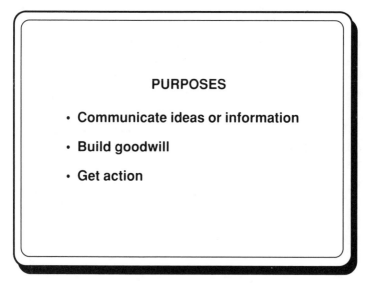

**THE PURPOSES OF
COMMUNICATING IN BUSINESS**

1. To communicate MEANINGFUL and USEFUL ideas or information to a (usually) specific audience.

2. To build goodwill.

3. To get action.

Every word that is used in a business communication — telephone call, interview, memo, letter — must meet one (or more) of these purposes. Otherwise time is being wasted for both the sender and the receiver.

POOR VISUAL

PURPOSES

- Communicate ideas or information

- Build goodwill

- Get action

IMPROVED VERSION

PROBLEMS WITH VISUALS

Three problems occur most frequently with visuals: 1) they are relied upon too much (our old friend with 80 slides in 60 minutes is a fine example); 2) they are too often just words and numbers, when a graphic could be created; 3) they are too complicated for the audience to grasp in just a glance. It takes a strong speaker to ignore the irrelevant aspects of a complex visual. That's how so many speakers get derailed.

POINTS TO REMEMBER

Create visual aids which help rather than work against you. Create visuals which reflect both the quality of your presentation and the quality you are selling, representing, or striving for.

The TO DO List:

Assess your current visuals. Be honest.

CHAPTER NINE

PREPARING BEFORE THE PRESENTATION

Room and equipment preparation are two aspects of making presentations that many people — even sophisticated professional speakers — neglect in their process of getting ready to speak. In the same way that you prepare your mind, your body, and your voice ahead of time (see the following chapters), make sure that you have done all that you can do ahead of time to insure the appropriate setting for your presentation.

Appropriate room arrangement and fully functioning audio-visual equipment are two keys to successful speaking. This preparation is necessary whether you're doing a committee meeting, a dinner meeting of your professional organization, or a major speech to a convention. As the speaker, you have not only an obligation, but a right, to do everything that you can do to maximize the success of your presentation or your part of the proceedings.

SCOUT THE ROOM

There are certain steps that you will want to take before the day or time of the presentation. One of those is arranging to have the room set up in the way you would like. Two is to request the audio-visual equipment that you will need. And three, if at all possible, is to see the room yourself, get a sense of its logistics, including its size and dimensions, where the screen is located in relationship to the audience, whether there's a platform that you will have to step up and down from, where the light switches are—features that you need to know ahead of time to make best use of the facilities.

The ideal approach is to be able to scout the room ahead of time—the day before, the morning before. Short of that, plan to arrive at least an hour before your presentation. Be sure that you know how to get to the location. Be certain you can find a parking place. Plan to carry your own equipment and materials into the room. Adjust the visual aids, adjust the screen, rearrange the room (because the chances are good it will not be arranged exactly as you had asked). Become adjusted to the size and shape of the room. Practice eye contact to the left side, to the back, and to the right side (even though there are no eyes there to look at). Project your voice: get a sense of the size voice that you will need to reach this audience. Decide if you will be forced to use a microphone. Having found out the size of the room and the size of the audience you will have a better idea of whether your existing visuals are large enough to be seen, or whether you need to have them enlarged. Check the light switches so that you can dim the front lights (or ask someone to dim them) if such is possible during the time that you will be showing certain visuals.

One of the other significant aspects about scouting

the room ahead of time is that you will have a mental picture of what you're going to be facing. This is an important aspect of taking care of everything ahead of time that you can. Assume you are going to address 200 people. If you walk into the restaurant and up to the speaker's table just before the dinner, the reaction that you are apt to have is, "Oh my goodness, this is a huge room. This is a huge crowd." The knot in your stomach tightens up. If you had gone to the restaurant the day before to see the size of the room and all the tables, your mind would have processed the hugeness and put it behind you. When you walk into the room filled with people, you will have expected them. This mental preparation is another piece of getting yourself ready ahead of time.

ARRANGEMENT OF ROOMS

One key area is, of course, the type of room and the arrangement of its furniture. Different kinds of room arrangements lend themselves to different kinds of presentations—and to different kinds of results. Insofar as you are able to dictate the way you'd like to have the room arranged, you should do so. One of the ways to do that, if the meeting is being held in a hotel or restaurant, is to check with the person who invited you speak. Let her know what kind of room arrangement you would prefer. Be specific and assertive. If you are arranging the meeting or the presentation yourself, then you make your own arrangements about how the room should be set up.

The most common room arrangements in public buildings are classroom style, banquet style, and auditorium seating. The other common arrangement is U-shaped. Each type of room arrangement has advantages and disadvantages, depending on what the session is to accomplish. Classroom style is the most common arrangement in hotels and restaurants. Classroom style involves long, thin tables with chairs on one side, all directed toward the speaker's area. One advantage of classroom style is that the room can hold many people, and all have a place to keep their materials and take notes. The main disadvantage of classroom style is that people are looking at the backs of those in the rows ahead of them. With this setup you are less likely to get good discussion and active participation. In this arrangement, if the audience is large, it's important to have aisles running the depth of the room between the tables so that you can walk back in among people during the presentation. By getting closer to them, you minimize the barrier created by the distance between you and a large audience.

The U-shaped setup is a wonderful arrangement, if the group is not too large, because the audience can be on the three outside sides of the U, looking at each other, but also looking at you. You can walk into the U and get close to the participants, eliminating the distance barrier. Another advantage of the U-shape is that it encourages good participation. People can see each other's faces, can act and react with one another. You can be part of the discussion at the same time you maintain control.

In sessions where a consensus is to be achieved, the best arrangement is a circle or a rectangle, around a conference table or a series of tables, or with the chairs arranged so everyone appears to be equal; even you, as the presenter or facilitator, are a part of the circle or the rectangle. When you wish to be first among equals, you simply stand, enabling you to draw sufficient attention to your authority or your position as chair.

Banquet seating is what you typically see at luncheons and dinner meetings. Round tables are good for small group discussion during the meal; but they make

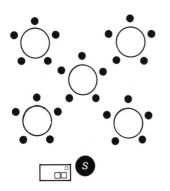

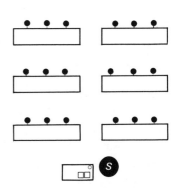

BANQUET   **CLASSROOM**

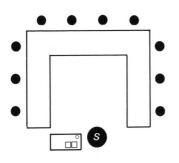

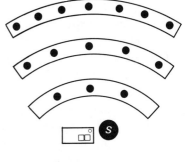

U-SHAPED   **AUDITORIUM**

it difficult for some members of the audience to comfortably see you when you begin to speak. The result is usually some awkward turning and scraping of chairs as you begin, to the detriment of your dynamic opener. If the moderator has indicated a five-minute break before your talk, people will have turned their chairs around before you begin.

Auditorium seating is, of course, for big groups. Auditorium seating is rows and rows of chairs, typically with no arms, with the rows going on forever. The advantage is that lots of people can be put into a reasonable-sized space, and they can still hear and see you and your visuals. One disadvantage is that there's no place for taking notes; if you expect people to write things down, they will have to write on their laps. The auditorium style seating arrangement also signals non-verbally "I'm going to talk and you're going to listen." Naturally you will find it difficult to get much discussion or involvement in auditorium style seating not only because of the size, but also because people are looking at the backs of the people ahead of them.

The non-verbal implications of these different types of room setups are important to consider. Speakers sometimes find that their presentation situations were not successful. Upon assessment, they discover that while the room arrangement signaled one kind of meeting, the speaker had another kind of meeting in mind.

Despite your asking that the room be arranged in a certain way, when you actually get to the room, you will discover very often that your request has not been implemented. One of the many reasons, as we discuss, that you arrive early (an hour early or at least a half-hour early) is to rearrange the room yourself or get the room rearranged in the way that you wanted.

ORDERING AND CHECKING AUDIO-VISUAL EQUIPMENT

That second vital aspect of preparation is checking on the audio-visual equipment. Audio-visual equipment creates many problems and these problems may unhinge the most confident of speakers. My experience in hundreds of speeches is that there is always potential for something to go wrong. And this is true even in large, expensive hotels which have clearly laid out a great deal of advertising and promotion to say that they are meeting and conference centers.

What should you request? A slide projector with carousel (if you don't have a carousel of your own) for your slides or an overhead projector; a screen; a flip chart or dry erase board and easel. (Find out if the screen is attached to the ceiling or can be moved to meet your particular specifications.) Ask for a small table for the front of the room for your notes and extra handouts.

MICROPHONES

If you are going to be forced to use a microphone because the audience is so large that your voice will not carry to all the people in the room, this particular piece of equipment needs a tremendous amount of checking and testing. One of the reasons that I seldom use a microphone if the audience is less than 150, for example, is that something goes wrong with microphones 100% of the time. No one needs to be told how irritating it is to have the microphone not work at all; feed back tweets and whistles; or screech loudly so that the audience holds its ears in pain. All of those problems are not only unsettling to the audience, they're also unsettling to you as the speaker. And they totally destroy your dynamic opener and any other attempt at a strong beginning that you have planned.

Can you imagine what would have happened to the Gettysburg Address if Lincoln had used a microphone: "Four score and seven years . . . *can you hear me back there? Oh, okay, I'll speak louder.* Four score and seven years ago our fathers . . . **tweet, tweet** . . . *oh, sorry, this microphone is so bad.* Four score and seven years ago our fathers brought forth . . . **eeek, eeieei, clack.** . . ." Needless to say, the effect of some of the most memorable words in all of public speaking would have been lost.

Most sound systems require the expert touch of a technician. Many hotels have an expert technician, but some hotels and most restaurants and meeting rooms do not. Frequently the audio-visual equipment is brought in from an outside organization and dumped. The technician either never comes or goes away after he has done a cursory check of the equipment. When you arrive, even if you arrive an hour ahead of time with ample opportunity to adjust everything, the chances are great that you will not be able to get the microphone to do what you want.

What do you want the microphone to do? You want it not to give feedback. You want it not to tweet or whistle. You want it not to crackle. And most of all, you want it to be adjusted sensitively enough that it will accept and amplify your well-developed voice range. You must test it. Put on the lavaliere mike, hold the cordless hand mike in your hand, or stand near the mike stand and try your full vocal range. Speak loudly, speak softly, speak rapidly and slowly, all the vocal qualities that you are going to have in your presentation. See if indeed the sound system is adjusted to accept all you want to do. As you can tell, we are asking a great deal of the system.

A good system should be able to give you all of these things, but getting it to is a tremendous problem.

Perhaps the worst problem of using a microphone is that it lulls you into a false sense of adequate sound. This false sense of security makes it more difficult to convince yourself to project the enthusiasm and the dynamism that you would like. If the microphone ever tweets or flutters as you raise your voice to emphasize a word, you will find yourself not emphasizing any words in order to avoid the squeaking or fluttering, and you will fall into the dreaded monotone; more reason not to use a public address system unless you are required to do so.

PROJECTION EQUIPMENT

Set up and test projection equipment when you arrive at the location, set the slides in the carousel, making sure that they are all upside down and backwards so that they will project the appropriate way on the screen. (It will be helpful to have them numbered, so that if they fall out, you can replace them easily.) Run quickly through the whole carousel to make sure that all the slides are in the right way. It may be funny to have a slide upside down, and it does cause humor, but it also can tend to be upsetting to your equilibrium and your poise.

Adjust the position and height of the slide projector. Make sure that the slides project properly on the screen. That usually requires tucking some ashtrays or books underneath the front of the projector in order to get the slides to project on the screen rather than partly on the wall behind. Position the slide table the appropriate distance from the screen. Many times after you have positioned it, someone will move it for some other activity before your presentation; take a moment to mark the carpet with chalk so that you can roll the cart confidently out to the appropriate position just before you begin your presentation. You do not want to have to spend time in front of everybody readjusting it.

Be sure that there is a spare bulb for the projector. Even the sophisticated speaker finds it difficult to proceed without slides after the bulb blows out. If you're going to use a remote cord, figure out the distance that you can walk away from the machine with the cord so that you will not pull the machine off the stand as you are enthusiastically discussing one of the slides.

The same process is necessary for adjusting your overhead projector. The biggest thing that can go wrong with an overhead projector, again, is that the bulb will burn out. If there is no spare bulb, request one. If you are relying on your overheads and suddenly can no longer use them, you are apt to be flustered and lose your poise, or worse, have your presentation fall to pieces.

If using a film, all the same cautions apply. Know how to thread the projector if the film breaks (or be certain there is someone close at hand who knows how: "Just call me on extension 234" does not work in the middle of your film). Be certain the distance to screen is established. Know how to turn the lights down or out (or arrange to have it done at the appropriate time). If using a videotape, check that the television monitors work, that they are placed so that all the audience can see a screen, and that the volume is tuned.

PODIUM

Avoid using a podium if you are able to do so. The podium is a barrier between you and your audience; like any barrier, it must be overcome during the course of

POOR

BETTER

your presentation. If you are short, most of your body will be covered up and that means most of the instrument that is your body will not be available for use. If you are tall, you are tempted to lean on the podium, or worse yet, loll across the top of it. Interestingly, this action represents an unconscious attempt to cross the barrier to get closer to the audience. It did represent such an attempt during a question-and-answer portion of a presentation that I saw several years ago. The speaker was excellent, a prominent urban service district board member. As a fine speaker, he sensed that he would like to have been closer to the audience in at least this less formal part of his presentation. His height enabled him to literally sprawl across the top of the podium—and he did! He would have been far better off to remove the mike from its stand and move about among the audience.

It is extremely difficult to gesture from behind a podium unless you are particularly tall. A podium also lulls you into a false sense of security that you are comfortable, and safe. That false sense of security soon has you clutching or leaning on the podium, and not gesturing at all. Soon your voice also moves into a particular kind of monotone. The action of gestures and motion helps keep your voice varied.

If there is a podium, ascertain whether it can be moved off to the side, removed entirely, or turned sideways. As with many things that I have suggested to you in this book, using the podium at the beginning of your speaking career or early on in your presentation-making is not a good habit to get into. It is a crutch. It will discourage you from learning to stand and move independently. Your body is an important part of your delivery. The podium hides this instrument. When you lose most of the motion and action that gestures create, you are making more work for yourself by needing a better voice to compensate.

You may think an hour is more time than you can allocate to this preparation activity. You'd be wrong. It's another part of getting everything ready that you can get ready ahead of time so that during the actual presentation you are concentrating solely on the material that you've prepared and on delivering it.

GETTING THE RIGHT INTRODUCTION

Another aspect of preparation ahead of time that will pay you wonderful dividends is getting the appropriate introduction for your presentation. Someone often will have asked you for some biographical information. What happens too often when you simply give them a resume, a biography, or your brochure is that the introduction is a lengthy list of all the less-than-significant places that you went to school, all the professional organizations that you belong to, and all the wonderful honors that you have won — material designed basically to bore the audience, to lull them into a state of lethargy which you will then have to break them out of. Unless you have interaction with the introducer ahead of time, your name is apt to be mispronounced. A third potential mishap is that the introducer gives your point or speech title away when you'd rather he didn't.

One of the other problems, particularly in professional, civic, or fraternal organizations, is that the introducer takes too much of your time, giving a little speech of her own, which detracts from you and your presentation. Finally, sometimes the introducer gives you such a build-up that you feel that you could never meet the expectations that he has set for you.

How do you get the right introduction? By preparing

it yourself, giving it to the person who is going to introduce you and asking him very charmingly to please use this introduction. If he indicates that he would like to add a few things, you should ask what things. Or you might simply say, "It would help my presentation and our success tonight if you would please use this introduction that I have prepared." This is a time to be a bit assertive.

What should your introduction include? That depends entirely on you. Some people simply want their name to be mentioned: "Please help me welcome our speaker for tonight, Marian Woodall." Some people want to have some specific item from their background mentioned because it relates to the audience, the topic, the reason that you are the qualified expert. Find something that ties you to the particular interests, purposes, or goals of the group to include in the introduction. People are more apt to accept you as a result of that tie. Select one or two items which are specifically related to why you've been asked to speak or what your connection is to this group. Perhaps you've written a book, won an award, chaired a committee, or are sponsor of a particular program. It's wonderful to have that be a part of your introduction. Include your title or your topic if you'd like the introducer to mention it, but you're under no obligation to do so.

Another aspect of your background which is often interesting or helpful in the introduction is some small piece about your past life which relates to the group in question. I was born and raised on a ranch in Idaho. When I speak to agricultural groups, rural co-ops, or ag-chem groups, I like to have some reference to the fact that I was born and raised in an agricultural setting. It's a point of identity. If you are addressing a group of athletes, you may wish to mention some athletic endeavor from your past — or present. Famous politicians always bring up their athletic prowess in any situation which is even faintly related to athletics or sports or fitness. Perhaps you won an award some time for something related to the particular organization. That would make a relevant tie-in.

What you do not want, generally, is the lengthy biography. People usually do not care where you went to school twenty-five years ago (or even five years ago). Generally speaking, audiences are not interested in your college major fifteen years ago. They are not impressed by the incredible number of organizations you have belonged to, or by the number of awards that you have acquired over the years. Should the introduction include your name? Perhaps yes, perhaps no. Your name may be well known to the group. Your name may be in the program or on the agenda. You may choose not to have them mention your name but in most cases, they should.

Assume that I'm going to address the Oregon High School Debating Society. The introduction that I have prepared to have the introducer use might go something like this: "Our goal tonight is to polish and sharpen our professional speaking skills. Here tonight to help us with that polish is a woman who has been a professional speaker for over twenty years. Her very first speech was a demonstration in high school to try out for the debating team. Please welcome Marian Woodall." That's three sentences, and three sentences is usually enough. You must, of course, consider the situation, the special considerations of a particular presentation; there may be times when much more is appropriate to say, but in general, briefness is best. You goal is to have the introducer get you up there without stealing your punch line, without distracting from your own shining qualities, without establishing something too challenging for you to live up to, and let you get on with your speech.

TOOL KIT

If you present frequently (or perhaps even occasionally) you will want to develop a small bag which is your speaker's tool kit. This little kit will include items that you are apt to need, including an extension cord (preferably one with a three-prong outlet), chalk, wide and narrow felt tip pens and dry markers, transparent tape, masking tape, small scissors, a few note cards, paper clips, yellow sticky notes (my favorite device), blank transparency sheets (in case you need to create something at the last minute), breath mints, aspirin or other headache remedies.

And perhaps a granola bar. One of the things that happens is you do not wish to eat much during the meal; after you finish, you are exhilarated, exhausted, and famished—and the food is gone. Have the kit ready at all times and keep it behind you when you speak. If you are a woman, you may wish to have some powder and lipstick, comb or brush.

POINTS TO REMEMBER

Prepared is ready. If you never have a problem with room arrangement or equipment, if you never need any item from your speaker's tool kit, you will be the first person in the history of speaking who has found everything completely satisfactory every time.

CHAPTER TEN

PREPARING YOUR MIND— MINIMIZE YOUR NERVOUSNESS

General agreement exists that effective delivery will do more to win an audience to you than an effective message. Ironically, however, it is a well-prepared message that enables a speaker to be confident enough to deliver effectively. Delivery is a natural process, not an artificial one: Your voice and your body will naturally complement and amplify your words—provided you let them. Confidence in your message enables you to let them. In fact, the best way to minimize nervousness is to be over-prepared. When you know both your general subject and your specific presentation cold, confidence is built in.

NERVOUSNESS IS NATURAL

Nervousness is one key aspect of public speaking

that most speakers are concerned about. It is important to recognize that some nervousness is not only inevitable, it's expected. And it can be positive, if you channel it appropriately. Whenever you are gearing up to do something unusual, something other than what you normally do, there is going to be some tension, some adrenalin flowing. That adrenalin is a positive quality. It's the quality which enables you to be "up" enough to start in high gear. If you do not have any tension or nervousness, my strong suspicion is that you probably are not ready to give the presentation.

Never resort to alcohol, over-the-counter calmatives, or drugs, thinking that they will help you with nerves. Dulling your senses minimizes any chance you have to be spontaneous, enthusiastic, and genuine. A genuine speaker will be accepted by most audiences, even if she shows nervousness; a speaker with his senses dulled will leave the audience unmoved, or worse, hostile. Crutches do not help you learn to be a better speaker. They do not even truly help you get through a single performance, if success is your goal.

ATTITUDE IS EVERYTHING

Your mind is the first of three instruments that you have to work with in delivering a speech (the other two are your body and your voice: Chapters Eleven and Twelve). Successful delivery begins with effective use of this first instrument—your mind. Successful delivery begins with attitude. Whether you think you are a good speaker or not, you're always right. It is your mind that establishes the quality of delivery that you are going to have.

If you recognize that presenting is communicating

and you have practiced communicating to groups of more than one, you should be able to say to yourself, "I can do this. I want to do this. This is important." At minimum, you must, absolutely must, quit saying "I hate to give speeches. I can't give speeches. I'm no good at this. This is going to be awful." Every time you express failure you reinforce the possibility of its happening. When you express (or even think) the fear, the symptoms of anxiety increase; these symptoms in turn increase the fear. Begin to break that cycle by resolving to think positively. Be your own best friend (not your worst enemy) when thinking about speaking to a group.

PRE-SPEECH WARM-UPS

You must develop an attitude which says "I can." Warming up before a presentation involves getting your mind ready as well as getting your speech ready. Getting your mind ready should begin at the same time preparing the speech begins: when you first get the assignment or decide to speak. Pre-speech warm-ups should begin weeks, at least days, before the presentation, not just hours before. (See Chapter Fifteen for "just before the speech" relaxer techniques.)

Here are some warm-up methods you might try to help you improve your confidence:

- Self-talk
- Affirmations
- Visualizing
- "Putting on your game face."

Self-talk includes reminders to yourself that this presentation is important, it's going to go well, you are prepared, you are confident. Self-talk banishes the negative things you used to say.

Affirmations work well for many people. A variation of self-talk, you create positive statements of worth or success such as "I am a good speaker and I am getting better." or "Speaking is a natural to me." Repeat an affirmation you have created until you believe it. Then it will be so.

A third approach to creating and using your pre-speech warm-up is visualizing. Visualizing is a technique which involves mentally playing through the presentation prior to giving it. Create a mental movie or videotape of yourself successfully giving the presentation. To practice visualizing, put yourself in a quiet room where there are no distractions and create a film of yourself — see yourself seated at the head table, sitting in the room, or standing near the front of the room while you're introduced; visualize yourself walking confidently to the front, establishing eye contact, delivering your dramatic first sentence, developing your thesis, presenting your oral guidelines, gesturing freely and comfortably; finishing your presentation with a strong close. Visualize the applause that will come when you're finished.

The result of visualizing is that you see yourself succeeding, increasing your confidence. It also gives you an opportunity to see which parts of the process you are most comfortable about and which parts need more work. What I find when visualizing is that there are certain phases that are harder to visualize; those are the points which need more attention. If I can go smoothly through the entire presentation in the visualization process, then I am confident I am equally prepared in all areas. But if I find myself pausing hesitantly in visualizing one part of the process, that's a signal that this is an area which needs more preparation.

The fourth approach to pre-speech warmup is what

athletes call "putting on your game face." In other words, getting yourself revved up. What the coach does in the locker room before the game is a little pep talk, "Let's go get 'em! We can do this! This is important to us!" kind of language. You need to have language like that to give yourself. This is different than self-talk in that it's the specific revving-up words in a revved-up tone to get yourself in high gear in the few moments (or half-hour) before the presentation. You want to begin your presentation in high gear. The audience is not likely to be patient while you get warmed up.

Putting on your game face involves getting the right mental attitude just before the presentation. Sometimes you work on enthusiasm in your car or on the airplane before you get there. You might just go into the rest room for a while, to make sure your hair is controlled and your tie straight, and to rev up your enthusiasm under your breath; you don't have to say anything out loud.

Imagine what would happen if a basketball player did not think about the game at all, but simply went out at the buzzer and tried to reach for the tip-off. Unless a player thinks about what he is going to do, thinks about his role in the game and his ability to contribute to the team effort, he won't be ready. Putting on your game face is exactly that, getting ready.

The enthusiasm, the excitement, the high energy generated during your speech must come first from you. The audience can never be more excited than you are, they can never have more enthusiasm than you have. Recognize that it's important to channel your nervousness in a positive way to create the enthusiasm. Let your nervousness help you to be the kind of speaker that you'd like to be. (More on this when we talk about preparing your vocal instrument in Chapter Twelve.)

POINTS TO REMEMBER

If you think you can, you can.

The TO DO List:

If nervousness has kept you from saying "yes" to a speaking opportunity, or if nerves have accompanied you to any presentation situations, begin TODAY to turn your mind around.

CHAPTER ELEVEN

PREPARING YOUR BODY

Your body is the second instrument that you have available for use when you're making a presentation. You make your body work for you by learning its natural positions. These natural positions minimize tensions and enable your body to work with you, projecting the confidence and enthusiasm that you know is inside it. A body that is not allowed to be natural will hold in tension, look frozen and stiff, or appear bored or uninterested. Be concerned about appearance, body posture and gestures, eye contact, and using your face in the most effective ways. Those five aspects of preparing your body each deserve individual attention.

POSTURE

The first and most basic aspect of preparing your body is finding and using correct, natural posture. Natural posture is upright, shoulders back, head high—but relaxed, not tense. Correct posture will allow you to breathe properly, making it easier to get your words out naturally.

There are several positions that speakers tend to adopt which are not natural posture; they not only inhibit your breathing and speaking, they are also inappropriate. The first is the fig leaf, in which your hands are clasped together in front of you at full arms length. Your clasped hands appear to be covering your crotch—inappropriate. The second is called parade rest, where your hands are clasped behind you at full arms' length, covering your fanny, giving yourself very straight shoulders and an exaggerated posture—inappropriate. Hands in pockets—inappropriate. All three are unnatural looks, the first two postures too stuffy, the last, too casual. However, the main reason they're inappropriate has to do with gestures. The problem with the fig leaf, parade rest, and hands-in-pockets positions is that you are trapping your hands. You are preventing them from making the gestures that they would automatically make to reinforce the words you speak. What should you do with your hands? Use the neutral position. See pages 144–145.

APPEARANCE

Appearing appropriate is essential. In general, you need to dress to the top of the audience that you're presenting to. Because you've assessed the audience, you realize there will be, for example, senior management people, staff people, and production line people. Your goal is to look similar to or as good as the top management people. That's true not only because they're apt to be the decision makers, but also because they expect you to be one of them. The people who work in less formal positions in the firm will not be put off by the fact that you are dressed up, but a chief executive, a president, a chief financial officer, will be put off if you look too casual.

One of the most embarrassing and easiest ways to lose your confidence is to show up for a presentation in slacks and open-neck shirt or in a dress with no jacket, and realize as you walk in the room that everyone is dressed up. Anytime you are in doubt about who the audience will be or what the dress should be, you always dress up, simply because it's an easy matter to take off your jacket, loosen your tie, take your tie completely off, or roll up your sleeves if the environment is such that you would look out of place in a three-piece suit.

How do you find out how the audience is going to look? In making the audience assessment, you have a good idea about it. You understand what kind of a meeting it is, whether it's a vacation or resort situation, an annual meeting being held in a downtown hotel, or a staff meeting being held in the company's cafeteria. What you don't know you should ask the person who contracted with you.

What would you do, for example, if you're going to Hawaii to present a workshop for a group and you are fairly certain they're all going to be in aloha shirts? You will not be in your aloha shirt. You are coming in as expert and as outsider. However, it is certainly appropriate to say to them, a few minutes into your presentation, "I seem to be overdressed here," or "Let's get down to work," and take off your jacket and perhaps your tie, relaxing your appearance a little bit. Recognize that it's always better to be a little overdressed than a little under-dressed. Recognize also that marketing proposals and business presentations require more formal, perhaps more conservative attire, for both men and women. Speeches to professional groups can sometimes be less formal, with presentations to civic groups and charitable organizations requiring still less formality. But we are generalizing. And the final decision is always yours, in accordance with your assessment of your relationship to the audience according to the Communications Triangle (see Chapter Two).

For men, the top of the line is a three-piece suit. Next down is a two-piece suit, then a blazer and sports jacket, all with ties. Next down is a sweater and an open-necked shirt. In terms of color, dark gray and navy are always safe, even in the summer, even in Hawaii. It's better to have a light weight suit which is not quite so somber for a warm climate, but you'll never be wrong with gray or navy.

For women, top of the formal line is a three-piece or two-piece gray or navy skirted suit, matching. Next down is an unmatched suit or a blazer and skirt. Next down is a dress and jacket. I can't imagine any situation where you would not want to wear at least a dress and jacket. A woman's ability to remove pieces if overdressed is similar to men's. Anytime you're wearing a jacket, after you've begun you can take your jacket off when that's appropriate to the situation.

How about shirt and blouse colors? White is always safe for men; pink, pale blue, pale gray, and tan are appropriate in many less formal situations. Anything other than those and you risk discomfort unless you know your audience extremely well, and they will be in plaid shirts.

For women, white or ivory are safe. Women have

a slightly greater opportunity to be colorful so long as they are careful in assessing their audience. Women can wear more colorful blouses; pastel colors look good in some situations, but they do not provide any statement of authority or strength. If brighter colors fit your personality, consider the situation and the audience, and wear them. In many situations women can wear colorful scarves so long as they do not overwhelm the wearer. What are the rules of thumb? You don't want your jewelry, your scarf, or your blouse to be the dominant statement. You, the speaker, are the statement and your clothes should complement you. Your entire appearance should complement the statement that your presentation is making, not overwhelm it. As you look in the mirror before you go out the door for a presentation, look at yourself as a stranger would. See if what catches your eye is the whole image, rather than the scarf, pin, or bright blouse.

Most women as professionals discover that as we gain more confidence in our presentations and in our professional manner, we can break the rules of somber suit, white shirt, and tiny tie. We can let our personality be expressed in our clothing in ways that are a bit more exciting. But it is important to always appear professional. You are always appropriate if you are conservative.

GESTURES

Gestures are a natural extension of language but your posture must allow the expression to occur. If your language says, "It's a great big problem," your hands want to make a big, sweeping gesture, if they are free to. If your voice says, "There was just a little, tiny cat sitting way over in the corner," your hands are going to point way over in the corner if they are able to. If your voice says, "There are three considerations we must make today," your hand is going to come up and show three fingers, if it is free to.

What to do? Learn and practice the neutral body position. The neutral position is simply to stand with your feet slightly apart, comfortably balanced, arms loose at your sides, hands resting lightly on the front of your thighs. (See the facing page.) Try it. When initially asked to stand in the neutral position, most of my clients say, "This is awkward; this is very uncomfortable. Oh, I can't do this." You may say the same; it's a position that you're not used to. Any time you're asked to do something new with your body, your muscles object. However, you're only going to be in the neutral position for a few seconds, literally. As you begin to speak, your hands will do what they would like to do to support your language.

Think of the neutral position as neutral gear in your automobile. You don't stay in neutral very long. You put the car in gear and move off. You return to neutral when you stop the car; you return to the neutral position when your hands have nothing to do. In order to achieve this appropriate neutral body posture, stand in front of a mirror. Look at fig leaf and parade rest and hands in pockets and see how silly and uncomfortable they look. Next, stand in the neutral position. Practice it. Continue to stand there even though it feels uncomfortable. But don't try to hold it for thirty seconds. You'll never do that and you'll never need to do that. Hold it for a few seconds, and then begin to speak.

Practice it every day. Practice it as many times as you need to, especially in front of a mirror, until your body comfortably falls into the neutral position without your having to think about it. That's the secret. Your body will soon learn to be comfortable in the neutral position and your hands will fall to your sides in a relaxed manner, ready to gesture.

POOR

BETTER

Simply put, your body needs to be upright and relaxed, and your hands need to be available (untrapped by clasping or pockets) to accomplish their gestures. If you are involved in the content of your presentation, your mind will not even think about the position of your hands.

The wonderful thing about gestures is that most occur naturally, as an extension of your language. If you feel that you have never been able to gesture and are concerned that using the neutral position and letting the hands go may not work for you, here are some ways that you can practice gestures to reinforce that they will occur.

Certain kinds of words encourage gestures:

- Number words—*first, second, third.*
- Words that indicate size—*the whole group, everyone, all of you, only those people on the left.*
- Direction words all encourage gestures—*top, bottom, left, right, all around me, behind me, clear up to the ceiling, way out to the left.*
- Adverbs encourage gestures—*slowly, rapidly, hurriedly, lazily.* Adverb words tell how something is done and you can very frequently supplement the how with a gesture of the appropriate feeling or mood.
- Verbs are motion words and also suggest gestures— he *raced* across the room, he *crept* slowly up to my desk, he *cowered* in front of me.
- Descriptions of people and of things—*it was just a mess, he stood in front of my desk like a little boy, she stood in front of my desk as confident as anyone I'd ever seen.* You can visualize what cowering at the desk like a little boy might look like and you can make your body do that. You can visualize what standing with great confidence in front of someone looks like and you can make your body do that.

Look through your presentation ideas for places to utilize these "gesturing words." You can simply practice them talking about nonsense if you want to.

EYE CONTACT

The fourth aspect of preparing your body is eye contact. This is definitely a skill. Many people love to look at eyes and are very comfortable doing it. Many other people do not. It is important that you give eye contact to everyone individually during the presentation. Naturally, if the size of the audience is 200, you can't give eye contact to every individual, but you can appear to be doing that. You look at different times to every section or piece of the room so that each group of people is included.

Some speech teachers used to advise that if you're nervous, you ought to look over the heads of people at something in the back. That is poor advice, for several reasons. First, it shows that you are afraid. Talk about having one strike against you as you begin! Second, eyes give you energy and support. People want you to succeed. Your friends in the audience, the people that you know, smile at you, they nod at you; they give you non-verbal encouragement, which is important in developing your confidence. Third, people do respond, even strangers, to what you're saying. They nod, they smile, they frown, they grimace. If you are not looking at them, you will not get the feedback that helps you know that you're doing a good job or that you need to find another approach. Finally, I know you've heard singers and musicians talk about how a lively, involved audience gives them energy and enables them to perform better. That same thing is absolutely true in speaking. If you are wound up and enthusiastic and excited and you give people good eye contact, they will give you back that excitement and enthusiasm 110%.

What if you have trouble with eye contact? Here's a simple exercise that you can practice ahead of time which will help you to conquer this problem. Ask a few friends (three is the minimum, I think) to sit with you or to stand with you in a small group. Arrange with each of them to give you a small hand signal when you have looked at them for three or four seconds. Then you tell a story. Talk about something you've done, or give your opinions about some issue. Present to them, communicate with them in a presentational way. Begin by looking at the first person and continue talking directly to that person until she unobtrusively signals you with her hand that you have spent four seconds with her. Then move onto to the next person. Look directly into that person's eyes and talk to him until he gives you the signal that you have spoken four seconds, and so on around the group.

After you've been from one to the next around the group a time or two, get more adventuresome and look first to one side, then the other side, then to the center. In other words, make eye contact randomly among the group of people. Do this as many different times as you need to until you are comfortable looking at people directly. Recognize that they do give you reinforcement, they mirror what you're saying, they give you encouragement, and they contribute to your confidence. This eye contact exercise is tremendously helpful if you have even the slightest problem giving everyone eye contact.

FACE

The fifth aspect of preparing your body is, of course, your face. And here again, there are some things that you can do ahead of time which will make you more confident that your face is going to do what you want it to do. The first aspect of your face that needs attention usually is the relaxed, neutral, or may we say, positive, face that you wish to have when you're seated at the head table before you're introduced or standing off to the side being introduced—any time that people may be looking at you, but you aren't speaking. And people are looking at you if they know you are to be the speaker. Appearing happy, relaxed, and confident before you are introduced matters a great deal.

Whether or not you realize it, a relaxed, happy, confident face is a difficult appearance to create for many of us. The older you get, the more difficult it is—because of gravity.

As you read this section, go into the bathroom or bedroom and find a mirror so that you can do the things I'm going to suggest. First of all, stand in a relaxed way; before you look in the mirror, compose your face in a neutral position. Now look into the mirror. You will probably discover that what you thought was a neutral looking face is somewhat hostile looking. The reason it's hostile is that gravity has pulled your facial muscles down, so the corners of your mouth are lower than the center. What you felt to be neutral appears negative or hostile. The older you get, the more this is true. Facial hair, especially a moustache, also pulls down the corners of your mouth.

What to do? Train your muscles to find a face that is neutral or positive in repose. A phrase which works to position your muscles appropriately is "cheese whiz."

Look in the mirror and say "cheese whiz." The muscles required to make the sounds, especially the "iz" sound of whiz, force the corners of your mouth up, leaving your lips slightly apart. What you'll find is a pleasant looking face in repose. Call it your relaxed, positive face.

When I first heard about cheese whiz, I was skeptical, and I said to myself, as you are probably now saying, "I can't go around saying cheese whiz all the time." You can say it more often than you realize. If you are sitting in a waiting room and the receptionist is looking at you, you want to have a pleasant look on your face. You can look down at your briefcase and say, "cheese whiz," under your breath. You don't have to make the sound, you just have to move the facial muscles. Mouth the words, and your face will assume that positive, relaxed position.

As I realized the significance of this face, I began to practice it consciously. Five or ten times a week I'm in a situation where I wish to have a relaxed, positive face, so I "cheese whiz" all the time. (By the way, if you're not a very photogenic person, you may find that saying "cheese whiz" gives you a much more attractive face in a picture than "cheese" does.)

One prominent situation in which you will want to have a relaxed and positive face is when you are seated at the head table. No matter what you are doing, there is someone in the audience who is looking at you. The same is true whenever you are seated prior to a speech, at a luncheon table, or while waiting for your turn during a panel discussion.

The other aspect of your face which is also important is that as you become relaxed and confident in your content, you will let your face do what it does naturally: smile, have a questioning look, or express strong feelings. The enthusiasm, the excitement that you have, the sparkle in the eyes, the tension in the face which shows excitement, will come naturally for most people, providing they are not frozen with nervousness. And as we continue to discuss and reinforce, the best way not to be frozen with nervousness is to be very confident of your material.

It's interesting that delivery matters more than content when you're making an impression, yet it's superb content that enables you to relax enough to have good delivery. There are a few professional people who can have good delivery and say absolutely nothing. We've all heard those kind of speakers, but they frustrate us in most cases unless they're entertainers or humorists.

Let me say again, confidence comes from knowing that your assessment is good, that you've prepared well — the content, your opening line, the oral guidelines, and a strong close. It's confidence in those qualities that enables you to be relaxed enough that the nervousness disappears and that during the presentation your body will do what you want it to by way of gestures. Your voice, as we'll discuss in Chapter Twelve, will also do what you want it to.

The essence of this is very simple. You do ahead of time everything that you can so that during the actual presentation, you can concentrate on delivering — which is the only thing that you can't do ahead of time (although you can practice the aspects of delivery as we are discussing).

POINTS TO REMEMBER

1. Knowing you look sharp and appropriate adds confidence.
2. Standing straight and tall demonstrates confidence; good posture is also necessary to let your body move naturally — which it will do if you let it.

3. Natural posture allows your body to mirror your words with appropriate gestures.
4. Real eye contact helps you to relax and draw energy from the audience; it also keeps the audience attentive.
5. Your face projects your enthusiasm through your smiles and other honest emotions.

The TO DO List:

To realize the extent to which you use both your face and your hands to gesture, put a mirror up near a telephone that you use frequently. Watch yourself as you talk. After just a few "looks" you will quit feeling self-conscious; notice how naturally you reinforce non-verbally what you express verbally.

CHAPTER TWELVE

PREPARING YOUR VOICE

The third and final instrument to develop to assist you in making effective presentations is, of course, your voice. Many of us are not very comfortable with what our voice sounds like when we hear it in our ears and even less comfortable when we hear it on audiotape. Do not worry too much about how it sounds. It never sounds to the audience the way it sounds to you. You **can** profitably use an audiotape of your voice to listen to your distracting voice mannerisms: "uh . . . ," "and ah," and so on. Of course, if you have gotten feedback that your voice is especially difficult in some way—it's squeaky, it's too low, it doesn't resonate at all—then you may want to consider some work to improve it.

The tones used to create good verbal sound are similar to the tones that create singing; while you need not be a singer to be a good speaker, you can learn the tricks to improve your voice and find your true tone. My own experience is perhaps typical. I had always had a terrible singing voice. In college I was so embarrassed about the sound of my singing that I would not go to church with a date; I would not stand beside him and subject him to my terrible voice. Some years ago, well into my speaking career, I ran across a little book called *Change Your Voice Change Your Life* by Morton Cooper. It gave me a single tool to use to develop vocal variety. I also learned to use my voice fully, without a microphone. Dr. Cooper indicates that most voices have more than one pitch level, a routine or habitual level and a natural level. He says that many people tend to use a pitch that is too low. The natural pitch allows us to control the sounds we make. This is an excerpt of Dr. Cooper's advice:

> Say "umm-hmmm," using rising inflection with the lips closed. It is vital that this "umm-hmmm" be spontaneous and sincere.
>
> The sound you are producing should be your right voice—this is your natural pitch, enhanced by tone focus.
>
> If you are doing exactly what I asked of you, you will feel a slight tingling or vibration around the nose and lips. This indicates correct tone focus, with oral-nasal resonance.
>
> If your pitch is too low, which occurs in most cases of voice misuse, you will feel too much vibration in the lower throat, and very little if any at all in the mask area.
>
> Repeat the exercise, say "umm-hmmm," to determine if you are doing it properly. Make a correction, if necessary,

until you feel the tingling sensation about
the lips and nose. . . . This is the voice
you will learn to use all the time. . . . This
should be your natural voice, your right
voice.

Try this simple technique. You might also speak to
a vocal teacher, or ask someone you know who sings,
to help you find the spot in your vocal range that is your
true tone. After you have found that spot, you will be
able to maximize your vocal instrument.

CREATE VERBAL GRAPHICS

To begin to recognize what you are aiming for in
terms of vocal variety or vocal color, think about your
voice as verbal graphics. Think about your computer
system: you have the ability to make words bold, to put
words in italics, to quote words, to underline words, to
set words off in capitals; all of these graphic variations
add visual interest to your reports, letters, handouts, and
brochures. If you can think of your voice as needing those
same kinds of special graphic techniques, then you will
be able to put the emphasis where you want it, to have
appropriate pauses, to let your voice tell the audience
through their ears what your written report would show
them with their eyes.

AREAS FOR DEVELOPMENT

You want to develop five qualities of voice:

- speed or pace
- pitch (highness or lowness)
- enunciation
- pronunciation
- inflection (or tone) and emphasis.

Many people say they have been accused of speaking too rapidly. Speaking too rapidly in itself is seldom a problem, because we can listen at four times the rate that people speak in normal conversation. The problem with rapid speech is that people fail to enunciate and pronounce clearly, fail to pause, and/or fail to have a varied pace in their voice. Speed should be varied. Sometimes you want to speak more rapidly, sometimes you slow the pace down, to make your voice more interesting to listen to.

Pitch is the high and low sounds in your voice. This is another tonal quality to add variety to your delivery. If you have been speaking at a normal pitch, when you choose to lower the pitch you signal to the audience that a change in content is occurring. Perhaps you are telling a story. Perhaps you are emphasizing a point. Sometimes you simply change these qualities to make the listening more interesting. Any change in pitch or speed will help the audience to return from their wool-gathering activities to tune in to you again.

Enunciation is the quality of saying clearly and distinctly all the syllables of every word. In our haste to speak in normal conversation, we often drop off the end of words. We slur together syllables or sounds in the middle of words. We often lose an entire syllable. A sample is "probly" instead of "probably," and "comferble" instead of "comfortable." We say "comin" instead of "coming," "goin" and "singin" instead of "going" and "singing." Enunciation is especially important if you speak rapidly.

Pronunciation means not only putting all the syllables in, but putting the primary and secondary accents or emphases where they belong. Naturally, it is important to pronounce all words accurately. Nothing makes you sound like an amateur — or worse, an outsider — quicker than mispronouncing a word, especially a word which is common knowledge in the group to which you are speaking. A word to the wise: When you are going to address a group, make it a point to check with someone knowledgeable to be sure that you are pronouncing absolutely perfectly all the words that are important or unique to that particular profession. Pronouncing appropriately and correctly is what the audience expects. Failure to do so will brand you as a dummy and you will lose credibility quickly.

The fifth quality is inflection. When you inflect a word, you change its tone to give it different meaning. The quality of inflection plus the quality of emphasis, which is making a word louder or stronger or firmer, are the two vocal qualities which are most interesting to practice and to use in presentations because we can change the meaning so dramatically. Even though these are vocal qualities, we can also call these qualities nonverbal because they change the meaning of the actual words in the same way that a gesture changes the meaning of a word which you use.

PRACTICE VOCAL COLOR

Below are two sets of sentences in which one word is bolded in each sentence. The bolding means that you should put particular emphasis on that word. The implied meaning in the parentheses after each sentence suggests the meaning to give the sentence. Practice these sentences with extra emphasis on the bolded word, even more than you would use if you were presenting. Pay special attention to the tone of sarcasm, secrecy, or gentleness, that you would use to create the meaning that is in parentheses.

I didn't tell John you were stupid. (Someone else told him.)

I **didn't** tell John you were stupid. (I'm keeping the fact a secret.)

I didn't **tell** John you were stupid. (I only hinted at it.)

I didn't tell **John** you were stupid. (I told everyone else.)

I didn't tell John **you** were stupid. (I said somebody around here was stupid. John figured out it was you by himself.)

I didn't tell John you **were** stupid. (I told him you still are stupid.)

I didn't tell John you were **stupid**. (I merely voiced my conviction you weren't very bright.)

You may be amazed at how easy this is and pleased to realize how readily you can transfer this inflection and emphasis process to your presentation to make your voice colorful, interesting and fun to listen to. Now try the second set.

He said he loves my sister.
He **said** he loves my sister.
He said **he** loves my sister.
He said he **loves** my sister.
He said he loves **my** sister.
He said he loves my **sister**.

Now that you have practiced the qualities of an interesting voice, practice the following sentences, giving them the different meanings suggested in parentheses.

Recognize what tremendous power you have to make the words come alive, what opportunity you have to demonstrate your true meaning, and what excitement you can add to your vocal instrument by being conscious of speed, pitch, enunciation, pronunciation, inflection, and emphasis.

1. Here comes the new computer. *(pleased, fearful, angry, neutral)*
2. You can get the project finished in time. *(as a question, as a neutral statement, as disbelief, as pleasure, as a threat, with confidence)*
3. Before you can take anything out, you must put something in. *(vary meaning by varying emphasis)*
4. This project can't be completed by your staff. *(vary meaning, vary emphasis)*
5. We'd be happy to talk with you about those concerns. Let's set up an appointment. When would be convenient for you?

The best time to practice voice development and these kinds of sentences is while traveling in the car. You can be as loud or assertive or emphatic as you want to. In terms of an actual presentation you will have written out your opener, your thesis sentence, and your conclusion; those three sentences, especially, need to be practiced—again, in the car or in an empty room if you can—so that you have wrestled with them enough and spoken them enough to know what kind of inflection and emphasis you want in order to maximize their effect on the audience. The other sentences that you would particularly want to practice ahead of time are the sentences which are your oral guidelines. There is a tremendous difference between a sentence which is inflected and emphasized perfectly and a sentence which is just spoken. Work on pauses and timing for these key sentences too.

Certainly, improving your vocal variety is a life-long process. Tape yourself doing these sentences. Tape yourself doing your entire speech. Listen with a special ear to other people who speak. Listen to good television and radio announcers. Learn as much as you can about how other people use their vocal instrument. Everything you learn will help you to maximize your vocal instrument.

WARMING UP

A second aspect to preparing your instrument is warming up your vocal cords in advance of a specific presentation. In the same way that singers warm up by singing scales and athletes warm up by stretching their muscles, you need to warm up your vocal cords, especially in two situations: if the room is large or the audience is big and you are not going to use a microphone, or if your presentation is longer than one-half hour. Warming up your vocal cords is easiest when you are driving to your presentation. Or warm up in your basement. You can also warm up in your hotel room. It is important to use your voice to express a gradually increasing range of sound. Your vocal cords will gradually become more flexible and able to accept comfortably the strain that you are going to put on them as you speak loudly, as you speak with authority, and as you speak for a long time.

When you are actually in the room preparing to present, your focus is the person in back of the room. Your goal is to be confident that you can project your voice fully to that last person. Have her in your sight and in your mind, and simply raise your voice sufficiently that you can assure her of perfect hearing. When you come to the presentation room early, you can stand in

the front of the room and practice finding the right projection which will reach the back row people.

What about microphones? As discussed in Chapter
Nine, microphones are a problem. The inexperienced
speaker is apt to want to use one in the same way that
she is apt to want to use a podium, as a crutch or an aid.
In huge rooms with large groups, or outside, you probably
do need a microphone, but the sound system creates
more problems in nearly every speaking situation than
it solves. Resolve to learn to do it right by developing
your voice rather than by relying on a microphone.

POINTS TO REMEMBER

The delivery of your presentation relates directly
to the success of your presentation. Focus your attention
on five qualities:

1. Eye contact which includes everybody or every seg-
   ment of the audience.
2. Voice projection that allows everyone in the room to
   hear all of your words, not just most of them.
3. Vocal variety that makes your voice so interesting to
   listen to that people do keep listening.
4. Enunciation so that each word is fully and clearly
   pronounced, adding its information to your total
   presentation.
5. Enthusiasm. No one in the audience is ever going to
   be more enthusiastic, more excited, more motivated
   by your talk than you are. That means that you must
   have the enthusiasm, the excitement, in your voice
   and in your body language from the very first sentence. That means that you must be at full speed
   when you first open your mouth.

The TO DO List:

Find an audio cassette recorder to capture your side of telephone conversations. Recognize the verbal color you already make use of.

While driving, practice the sentences for inflection and emphasis (or create some of your own). Force yourself to be extreme; broaden your range.

Practice "umm-hummm."

CHAPTER THIRTEEN

USING VISUAL AIDS EFFECTIVELY

Visuals are aids in your presentation. You are the star. The major problem with speakers who use audio-visual aids is that they tend not to remember this simple fact. Because of lack of awareness or perhaps nervousness, speakers let the audio-visual aids take over the presentation. They create too many visual aids (usually slides), and then they let the slides carry the load. What they're presenting is a talking slide show rather than a speech with a few well-chosen slides, foils, or charts to demonstrate key points or highlight the major aspects in the presentation.

Therefore, the first step to using visuals effectively is to be certain that they are chosen so that you can use them, rather than allowing them to use you, or to overwhelm you. (See Chapter Eight.) The second step is to use them appropriately. Your visuals will generally fall into one of three categories: projected aids, extemporary visuals, or physical objects.

GUIDELINES FOR PROJECTED AIDS

Projected aids include slides, overheads, (also called foils or overhead transparencies), videotapes, and films. First, make sure that you know how to operate all the equipment (or arrange for someone to operate it for you); second, adjust everything ahead of time. As noted in Chapter Nine, you will come to the location well in advance of the time of your presentation. It is absolutely vital that you make sure that all equipment is on site and that it is all working. Make sure that the projector is the right distance from the screen to maximize the size of the visual, make sure that the extension cords will reach.

Murphy's law is in effect 100% in speaking situations. If something can go wrong, it will. In the several hundred presentations that I have made in the past few years, something was potentially wrong nearly every time. It is always necessary to adjust, improvise, or change plans. For example, you're speaking at a dinner meeting. You came early to arrange the distance of the slide projector from the screen; you adjusted the angle of the screen. Just as you are sitting down to eat, you notice that a waiter has moved your slide projector table off to the side. You will now be forced to find the spot again, reposition the table, and re-focus the entire project in front of a waiting audience. You would have prevented this time-consuming and disruptive re-adjustment problem if you had marked the carpet with chalk from your tool kit so that you would know how far out to pull the slide table when you were ready to present.

It's not humorous to have the slides upside down, backwards, or the adjustment out of order at the time you begin your presentation. Both a dynamite opener and the dramatic delivery of that opener are lost or wasted if you pop up that first overhead or slide and it is incorrect. Run quickly through the entire tray of slides before the audience arrives (or while they are milling around with drinks). Similarly, check that your overheads are in the appropriate order. An "Oops, wrong visual!" can undermine your confidence during your presentation.

Second, be at the screen to use your visual, not at the projector. There are several reasons that this position is important. The most vital one is that the audience is going to be looking at you because you are the speaker; the audience is also going to be looking at the screen because the screen is a bright, well-lighted spot in the room. If you are not near the screen, but are standing in any other position in the room, the attention of the audience will be divided. The other major reason to stand at the screen is that you are reminded to use the visual. As part of a consultation with a client for a specific project (to coach *their* client), I was asked to videotape and critique a senior member of a public relations firm. He presented fifteen minutes of a media session that he had given the previous day. With slide projector remote control firmly in hand he proceeded to speak, flashing up slide after slide — with never a specific reference or comment to the content of the slide itself. My first comment in the critique was in the form of a question, "What were the slides for?" Recognition dawned on this astute gentleman that not only had he failed to use the slides appropriately, they had competed with him at every moment of the presentation.

The third guideline for slides or overheads is to use your hand (palm out, fingers extended) to point to the spot on the screen where you want the audience to look. If you want them to look at the heading, at a particular part of the diagram, at the totals near the bottom, you so indicate by pointing to those areas. In that way, you control the audience's eye contact with the visual. Many people use a pencil, a pen, or a telescoping pointer to point to the screen. Those items all have their drawbacks because when they are not pointing they turn out to be playthings, to jiggle, click, or telescope in and out—all without your realizing it. There's nothing wrong with a pointing tool, so long as you remember to lay it down each time (or most of the time) after you finish pointing. That is difficult to remember. The best approach is to learn to do it right: use your hand.

When you introduce the visual by turning the slide projector on, clicking the remote control, or placing the overhead on the screen and then turning on the light below it, you want to immediately explain the content of the visual. Summarize it. Give its significance. Immediately demonstrate what point it is making. Then pause, to give the audience time to absorb what you've said and to look at the rest of the visual. Do not talk while they are absorbing the visual. As you continue to use the visual, demonstrate with your hand, as well as with your voice, what is important about it. If the room is huge and the screen is too far away for you to walk back and forth to it, you may be able to acquire a laser pointer. Be careful to lay it down between uses or practice enough that you do not play with it, either.

One final possibility when you are using overhead transparencies, no matter where the screen is placed, is to learn to disclose the items using a half sheet of paper as a cover for the transparency. You pull the paper down one line at a time as you begin to talk about the information on that line. It is also possible—though expensive —to have your slides prepared so that each one adds the next line of information. Each slide will typically be presented first in its entirety; the second slide presents the title and first point; the third slide, title plus points one and two, etc. This approach achieves the same effect as disclosing on a transparency. The greatest disadvantage, aside from cost, is the number of slides you are required to have.

Finally, make the visual disappear when you are finished referring to it or when you are not referring to it. It's easy to make transparencies disappear; you simply eliminate the light source: move to the machine and turn it off. With slides, you need black slides between each slide so that when you click the remote control what comes up on the screen is nothing. Eliminating the light is important because the huge white light in the room will detract from you as the center of attention and from what you have to say. All of these uses of slides and overheads require practice, and you will want to rehearse with the specific overheads or slides that you are using so that you are comfortable with timing and placement (See Chapter Fourteen).

Using films and videotapes is easier. Most of the time you will want to provide a preview of the material, naming the highlights, indicating specific aspects to watch for, to help the audience get fullest use of the visual. Remember that you have seen the film at least once before; they will be seeing it only once. Sometimes a film visual has best dramatic value if the topic is not previewed; in those instances, offer highlights or summarize the important aspects after the showing. It is unwise to assume that everyone will have the same impression or feeling that you have — or that you want them to have. People's reactions vary greatly based on their own experience. After your summary some still may have different feelings, but they will at least understand your point.

A note about eye contact while using visuals: Be sure to talk to your audience, not to the visual. Everyone has been in audiences where the speaker spent most of his time with his back to us talking to the screen. The rule of thumb is "No eye contact, no voice." In other words, do the adjusting and the walking that you need to do silently. Look at the visual to get your perspective, place your hand where you want it, turn around toward the audience, and then begin speaking. The audience is patient. They will wait for you. They do not expect you to be talking every moment. In fact, the pauses help them gather their thoughts, process their reactions, and prepare for the next point. Do not be afraid of pauses. Do not be afraid of silence.

GUIDELINES FOR EXTEMPORARY VISUALS

Extemporary visuals include chalk boards, dry erase boards, blackboards, and flip charts.

First, start with a clean, blank space. If someone has presented before you, make sure that the space is clean before you get up to speak. Anything written will distract from your opener, your oral guidelines, your introduction.

One of the reasons that people use flip charts, as opposed to chalk boards or dry erase boards, is that they have the opportunity to prepare the extemporary visuals ahead of time. This "create ahead" approach makes them semi-extemporary, but they are usually easier to read and easier to handle. Talking, writing, and listening are a little bit like juggling. Not all of us do it well. When you write your extemporary visuals ahead of time, be sure to write on every other page, so that there is white space, which is all that the audience sees until you are ready to turn to the particular page that you want.

You have two other choices besides writing your extemporary visuals ahead of time. One is to ask for a scribe. He can write while you facilitate the brainstorming with the audience which usually creates what you want written. The other option is to stand sideways to write. The rule again is, no eye contact, no voice. If you do the writing yourself, keep your mouth shut while you're writing, until you are turned back to the audience.

Print if you can. Most of us have better printing than writing. Use large, simple letters. Abbreviate whenever abbreviations will make sense to the audience, especially if you are writing as you go. Once again, make it disappear when you are not referring to it. Turn the sheet over. Leave a blank white space ready for your next inscription.

GUIDELINES FOR PHYSICAL OBJECTS

When using objects as visuals, be certain that they are large enough that the audience can see the details you are pointing out. Otherwise, plan to move out among the audience, holding the object aloft for as many people to see as possible.

Sometimes speakers are tempted to pass around small items for individual scrutiny. This approach gives people a chance to examine an item carefully and there is some merit to that possibility. The negative aspect is that quite a bit of attention will be taken away from you and your presentation, while the item is being passed from hand to hand, while individuals are examining it, and as one person is moved to make a comment or discuss the item with her neighbor. Get the idea? It is better to have the item available for people to examine after your speech than to pass it around while you are speaking.

WHAT ABOUT HANDOUTS?

Some form of handout is an essential part of any talk, speech, presentation, or public address (with the possible exception of acceptances for honorary degree presentations and other honors). The simplest handout is an agenda or outline of your highlights. This item typically is either reprinted on your letterhead or individualized by photocopying the group's logo on the top of the page, your logo and address on the bottom. This is clearly a subtle marketing device. You may choose to hand this agenda out after your talk, but the general rule is to have it in the hands of the audience prior to or at the same time as you begin. If the agenda or handout is extensive, after your opener you might stop so that people can glance through it quickly. Ask them to scan it, and be quiet while they do.

Technical presentations and business presentations often require more extensive handouts. If the size of the group permits, hand out unbound sheets individually as you come to that material. Sometimes handouts are bound into a small booklet. The problems multiply as the number of pages multiply. On the one hand, if people have something to read they are apt to read rather than listen. On the other hand, if they have something to follow, they are apt to pay closer attention and grasp more of what you say. The solutions vary. If there aren't too many pages you can ask people to scan the booklet quickly (as with the agenda), remaining quiet while they do. This action is best handled right after your dynamic opener, sometimes even before your oral guidelines. Once their curiosity is satisfied, most will pay attention to you. If the booklet is too long for that approach, you can let people know that you will stop at the beginning of each new page to allow a quick scan. Then proceed with the details.

A third approach, best if the booklet is extensive or if there is a huge audience, is to tell the audience that complete handouts are available at the door after the presentation. On the surface this seems to be the best idea for all occasions; however, there are two weaknesses: many people like to take notes; people will follow you with more understanding if they are given a preview. Assess your documents, the type of audience, your assertiveness and control as a speaker, and make the appropriate decision.

POINTS TO REMEMBER

1. Use visuals to support your words; do not let visuals overwhelm your message.
2. Break the news of the entire visual when it first appears; give the audience time to absorb what you have just revealed.
3. Guide the audience to important aspects of the visual.
4. Pause to let the audience catch up with you.
5. Make the visual disappear when you are done with it or not using it directly; don't let it compete for audience attention.
6. The visuals are not the star; you are.

CHAPTER FOURTEEN

PRACTICE, PRACTICE, PRACTICE

As must be totally evident by now, successful presenters do not wing it. No matter how well you know the material, no matter how much of an authority you are, no matter how many times you have spoken on a topic, some special preparation is necessary for every situation if you wish to have the material individualized and specific to that group or situation. Some practice is also necessary regardless of how successful or professional a speaker you are.

PRACTICE THE STRUCTURE SENTENCES

Special attention to your opener, your thesis sentence, your oral guideline sentences, your conclusion, and your second conclusion will pay dividends far beyond the extra time that you spend practicing those pieces. You can practice each of these parts separately. If you are a novice at presenting, use your note cards and practice the entire presentation several different times. Practice it while you're out for a walk if you're walking in a relatively isolated place. Practice it in the shower or bathtub. Practice it down in the basement or in the garage. You can always practice it in my favorite spot—driving in a car. If you are delivering a manuscript presentation, practice it with special attention to raising your eyes (for eye contact), pace, pauses, and emphasis. Deliver it, don't read it, even in practice.

If there are certain illustrations or stories, anecdotes, descriptive pieces in the speech, practice those separately from the whole presentation too. At least one practice needs to be timed, using the note cards, going from beginning to end without any breaks, to be sure that you fit the time frame that you are being asked to present in. Remember that in the actual presentation, as your enthusiasm heightens and you truly get involved in your presentation and in your audience, things are apt to expand. Prior to this type of development and practice, you may have discovered that your presentations were shorter than you thought they would be. Chances are that you hurried. However, as a result of this preparation and practice, you will find that your presentation expands. The stories will get a little longer. You will remember and say things from the 98% that you had not planned to say.

You should also practice by presenting your material into an audio cassette player, playing it back and listening to it carefully. This process is apt to be somewhat startling at first, but then a most instructive experience. You can learn a great deal, of course, about your voice, your timing, your pauses, as well as about the material itself.

If the presentation is sufficiently important to you

personally, practice it in front of a video camera. Look at yourself. See what others see. If you have not seen yourself on videotape before, the first time through you should watch the tape simply to get a sense of how you look. The first few minutes are apt to be revealing, startling, and sometimes a little painful. As you continue viewing, you will get used to what you look like, and you begin to focus on the material. The second time through the shock value is behind you. You can be objective and critical, both about the good things that you do and about the things that you need to improve upon.

PRACTICE WITH VISUALS

Whatever visual aids you are using, include them in at least one session which is a total run-through. Your concerns are placement, timing, and gestures. For placement, where are you positioned in relation to the visual (beside the screen for overheads and slides; beside the flip chart; behind the table-top chart; holding up the model). Timing factors include these: at what point will you point to it, and how long will you keep it in front of the audience. Finally, practice what gestures will accompany the visual while it is on display: side of hand pointing to the line or part being discussed; sweep of arm to indicate the entire drawing or model; pull-down of cover sheet to disclose the transparency points one by one.

The effect of quality visuals will be lessened if you are awkward using them. Your facility with visuals will improve each time you use them, and successful use further enhances your upward spiral of confidence.

Only you know how important it is for you to develop your skills as a presenter. For each individual situation, make a determination about its significance, then resolve to spend the amount of time, not only in development, but in practice, to achieve the goal that you want.

Each time you deliver a presentation you are growing. Every time you present, if you present for many years, hundreds of speeches, you will continue to grow. One of the most exciting part of presenting material in a professional way is that there is always room for improvement. Make certain that you DO grow; as a part of your regular post-presentation process, debrief yourself immediately after a talk (or as soon as you can). Evaluate yourself on both the good aspects and the aspects that you want to change or improve upon before the next presentation. Jot down everything you can think of. Keep these self-evaluations in your speech file. And when you repeat the same presentation, or a similar one, you have an even greater opportunity to improve through the debriefing. That improvement is satisfying and rewarding, both personally and professionally.

POINTS TO REMEMBER

There is nothing wimpy about practicing. All the best people do it! The professionals in any profession practice. Professional speakers practice. You will practice too, if you want to succeed.

The TO DO List:

Isn't it obvious!

CHAPTER FIFTEEN

BEGINNING TO SPEAK

You are prepared: presentation and appearance both appropriate to the audience, game face on, visuals ready, and equipment positioned. Yet you still have butterflies? Of course you do. The goal, as we say, is just to get them all flying in the same direction! Pre-speech tension is both natural and necessary; the key to successful delivery is to channel that tension to work for you. Here are tips for re-directing this last-minute nervousness.

TIPS FOR RELAXING
JUST BEFORE YOU SPEAK

As you are waiting to be introduced you can unobtrusively do one or several of these relaxers:

- Do a few simple isometric exercises while seated to force your muscles to relax. Clench and unclench your fists. Grip the sides of your chair firmly, release, repeat.
- Drain tension out of your arms (in the rest room or out in the hall) by dangling them at your sides. Practice what athletes do: shake your wrists or twirl them and wiggle your fingers. You'll reduce your tension and increase circulation too. A few deep knee bends will also loosen your body.
- Take many deep, deep breaths. Exhale each breath slowly. You can learn to do this without drawing attention to yourself even while seated. Up to two minutes of deep breathing will increase blood circulation and ventilate your body.
- Walk briskly up and down the hall.
- Move your shoulders up and down. Pretend there is weight on them that you must shake off. Shake it off.
- Give yourself one final pep talk: "Let's do it!" "Go get 'em!" "I'm excited!"
- Remind yourself one final time that you are the expert: no one in the room (generally) knows as much as you do about the topic; that's why you were asked to speak.

In order to have your mouth be as comfortable as it can be, avoid drinking milk or eating dairy products (which create mucous) before your presentation. Avoid caffeine in coffee, tea, or cola soft drinks because it adds to your jitters. Avoid cold drinks such as iced tea or the glass of ice water sitting in front of you at the table because those will chill and tighten up your vocal cords. The best drink is hot water or mild hot tea. In fact, when the program chair approaches you before the presentation and says, "Is there anything else I can do for you?" respond, "Yes, I'd love to have a cup of hot water." Of course avoid alcohol.

PLACING YOUR NOTES
OR YOUR MANUSCRIPT

When you are able to place your notes or note cards ahead of time on the small table at the front of the room, do so. Make certain that they are in exact order, the introduction card on top. The exception would be if you are still studying them at the last minute. As you speak you will lay each one aside. Do not flip it over or put it to the bottom of the stack.

When you're presenting a manuscript, find an opportunity to lay your manuscript out — open to the first page if possible — on the podium in advance. When you are walking up, you will not have to carry it with you. Because it is laid out, open, you can slip it quickly up to the top of the podium before you establish eye contact. The business of shuffling through a file folder, creaking open a notebook, or rattling pages of paper is unsatisfactory: It calls too much attention to the manuscript. If you must carry it with you, keep it in your left hand so that you are able to shake hands with your introducer if a hand is offered.

If you're speaking after a breakfast, lunch, or dinner meeting, you will be seated while the serving and eating is going on, so your tension is apt to increase. Find out for certain at what point you're going to be introduced, then excuse yourself to the rest room or to the hall to employ some of the above tips for relaxing. Test your vocal cords if you can, take one last opportunity to get yourself revved up. Then come back in, take your chair, be introduced in just a few moments, and you will be certain to be up to speed with the first sentence.

USE YOUR SEATING POSITION
TO ITS BEST ADVANTAGE

The worst place that you can be asked to sit prior to being introduced is at the head table right next to the podium. The first problem is that you probably will be forced to use the podium because it's stacked on top of the table. The second problem is that you have no opportunity for that final movement to get your body loosened up before you begin to speak. The best place you can sit before a presentation is as far away from the front of the room as possible: after you are introduced, you make the walk to the front of the room, relaxing yourself, loosening your muscles, letting your tensions continue to drain away, and getting the attention of the audience as you move. Walk with purpose, head and shoulders erect, confident. Speaking is power; show that power in your movement.

If you are seated near the front of the room, take your time getting up, pushing in your chair, moving to the front of the room, all so that you can get your muscles moving and direct your energy toward your purpose.

If you are standing prior to your introduction, stand as far away as is reasonably possible so that you can take advantage of that chance to move to the center. From wherever you come, move with confidence. When you get to the center, stand with your body in its natural position and your hands in a neutral position. Establish eye contact with at least three or four people in different parts of the room. Wait, wait, wait. The audience is anticipating you. The more you ask them to wait and watch you, up to a reasonable point of course, the higher their anticipation builds. What you are doing is collecting yourself, centering yourself, establishing contact with yourself and with them.

THE OPENER

The first sentence out of your mouth is that strong opener. If it goes well, the entire presentation is apt to go well. Remember to pause, not only before you begin to speak, but also after that first sentence. If your opener is a question, pause an especially long time to let the audience think about the question, to let them absorb its significance. If your opener is a quotation or a statistic or a vital statement, pause to let that information sink in. Timing is everything here. Comedians rise or fall on the success of their timing. Timing is just as important for speakers, and the key place for superb timing is in your opener.

In the opening moments of your presentation you will want to be conscious of using especially big gestures and an especially big voice. Three good things will come from this beginning. You make sure that everyone can hear and see you. That's good for the audience. You will also be channeling any nervousness into positive energy. Finally, you will be establishing the pattern that you mean to use; your voice will continue large and your gestures will continue big throughout the presentation.

BEGIN

Whether you have notes or a manuscript, before you begin, use the same long pause, the measured eye contact, and the deliberateness that good speakers use. Draw a good breath but wait until you are ready. Silence is your friend. Smile. Deliver that strong opener just the way you have practiced it — with enthusiasm and strength. Mean it. From then on, it's easy.

DELIVERING YOUR MANUSCRIPT

As you begin to **deliver** (not read) your manuscript, eye contact is vital. You will find that you need only glance at the page to get the next phrase. One common problem with manuscript delivery is that people use looking down at the page as a crutch, missing many opportunities for eye contact. You can always have perfect eye contact when you are giving your name, the name of your company or organization (as well as much other basic information). Yet everyone has seen speakers who could not or would not even establish eye contact when they said "Good morning."

As you get near the bottom of a page, look ahead so you can finish the phrase or sentence at the same time that you slip the page off to the side (usually with your left hand). Don't turn them over and don't try to keep them in order. If one falls to the floor, leave it—unless it's a page you haven't delivered yet. (And resolve to do the speech extemporaneously next time!)

POINTS TO REMEMBER

1. Channel your tension to work for you, not against you.
2. The first few seconds of silence before you begin are vital, for both you and the audience. Make the most of them, with confident posture and excellent eye contact.
3. The first sentence out of your mouth will set the tone for your confidence, your delivery, and your success. Be doubly prepared with that first sentence, its words and its timing.

CHAPTER SIXTEEN

MAXIMIZING THE QUESTION & ANSWER SESSION

The question and answer session (Q & A) is a part of your presentation—an important part. Many fine speakers do well with the message and the delivery, but fall apart when they get to the question and answer session. This disaster occurs partly because they have not put in the same preparation for that vital piece of their work that they put in for the rest of the speech. Especially if you are giving a speech as an expert, your ability to respond to individual questions from the audience is often even more important than your ability to present the body of material in a unified way.

The first step in this part of the presentation is to have assessed your audience to establish beforehand what kinds of questions you should anticipate. One of the ways you do this is by thinking about the 98% of what you know that you do not say. You have chosen for a particular reason to present a particular 2%. There

will be people in any given audience whose greater interest is in some other material. For example, if you are
dealing with a controversial topic and you have decided
to take a neutral road or a position on one distinct side,
there are going to be some people who would like to
express their views. Other people will want to know your
views about the other side, a consideration, or an aspect
that you chose not to talk about. And those people usually wish to be heard.

THE PURPOSE OF THE Q & A

The basic purpose of the question and answer session
is to get as many people involved in your presentation
as possible. If you are a presenter who speaks, allowing
the audience only to listen, the chances are that you have
made a less distinct impression on them than if you had
involved them in some way. Remember, communication
happens only when the audience or the receiver receives
the message. That doesn't mean they necessarily agree
with it, but that they receive it, they hear it in their mind
as well as in their ears. If you have done a satisfactory
job of presenting your material, people usually want to
continue their involvement. They want to continue to be
part of the process. So, if the purpose is lots of involvement, your goal is to allow as many people as possible
to ask their questions.

RESPOND BRIEFLY

To get many people involved via questions, you
need to answer each briefly. There is a real temptation

when answering questions following a speech to give another speech; we all have sat impatiently waving our hand while the speaker went on and on in answer to one particular question. This is a frustrating wait for an audience and they may drift away, mentally and sometimes physically. However much good will and involvement you have created during the presentation, if you answer questions exhaustively you deny many other people the opportunity to ask their questions. You will have turned a potentially positive audience into a hostile or frustrated audience. A second reason, if you need one, for answering questions briefly is that the more you say, the more likely you are to get into trouble if people ask you questions that are technical or hostile.

Another temptation when responding to a question is to give another huge chunk of information that you chose not to give during the speech. Resist this temptation. You picked the 2% after careful assessment. Stick with it. Do answer questions using the 98% that you chose not to include in your speech; but resist the impulse to give a great deal of extra information. Resist the impulse to develop points that did not fit into your basic presentation. Stay with the thesis that you began with.

Many speakers wonder whether to ask for comments in the question and answer session. The best approach is to say, "What questions may I answer for you or what comments would you like to make?" A good speaker considers her situation and realizes there are other people in the audience who have strong and valid opinions and observations; that speaker wants to feel herself strong enough to be able to allow some of those opinions and observations to be stated. In other words, it should not be only questions that they ask and answers that you give. Genuine communication happens when people express opinions and feelings. There certainly is a potential for you to get into trouble, and as you read the sections on

handling difficult questions in Chapter Seventeen, you
will discover some techniques and tips for dealing with
people who have their own agendas and people who are
out to sabotage you. Basically, have a positive feeling.
When you offer to take comments in addition to questions, you invite some dialogue.

GETTING IT STARTED

How do you get the Q & A going after "What questions may I answer or what comments would you like to
make?" Step one is to pause, and pause some more, and
pause some more. Pause four or five times as long as
it feels comfortable doing; the audience needs time to
absorb your conclusion and time to get its questions developed. People in the audience have not said anything
for some time, and they want to be sure that what comes
out of their mouths is well phrased. (Put yourself in the
audience and remember how strongly you feel about
wanting to phrase a question appropriately.) The pause
is necessary to allow people to develop their questions.

What if there are still no hands raised after your
long pause? Three other tips that you might employ: one
is to ask a question of your own. Simply continue by
saying, "Let me ask you a question," and get a dialogue
going that way. Get a response from people. If you're a
genuine communicator and you care about your topic,
you are interested in how the audience feels. This is often
your first opportunity to get some verbal feedback to
supplement the non-verbal feedback that you've gotten
throughout the presentation.

Another approach to encourage questions or involvement is to say something like this: "A question people

often ask is. . . ." State the question and go on to answer it. Or you might say, "Your president asked me as we were sitting down to dinner. . . ." Give the question and answer it. Or "As I was coming in to speak this evening, someone asked me why . . . ," and answer it.

A third tip for getting the audience warmed up for this slightly less formal part of your presentation is to bring up something briefly from the 98% that you chose to leave out of your speech. Saying, "Another aspect of interest . . ." also allows you to bring up something that you wanted to mention but forgot, or some point you would like to reinforce.

What if after pausing, asking a question, repeating a question you're asked, and bringing up another point, you still do not have a question from the audience? It doesn't matter. You have given the audience lots of opportunity. You have filled the space with words and with conversation; you can simply pause again and say, "Are there any other questions I can answer for you, or is there anything else anybody would like to say?" If there's nothing, no one is uncomfortable.

What is this talk of discomfort? When the speaker says, "Are there any questions?" and there aren't any, the audience is a little uncomfortable, and they wish someone would ask a question. The speaker is typically uncomfortable and he usually shows it. He fidgets a little bit and thinks to himself, "Oh, I must have been a terrible failure if there aren't any questions." The speaker may grimace uncomfortably or make some offhand remark which nearly always reduces his level of professionalism, something like, "Oh, I guess I must have said everything there was to say." Or, "Gee, I thought there'd be questions." An inane comment which shows lack of confidence, lack of poise, puts an unpleasant ending on what may have been a very satisfactory presentation. However, if there are no questions the second time you ask, it doesn't make any difference because the requisite amount of post-presentation chitchat will have occurred.

ANSWERING THE QUESTIONS

See Chapter Seventeen.

GETTING IT STOPPED

Assume there are questions and you have answered them briefly, charmingly; you've followed the strategies of Chapter Seventeen for thinking on your feet. At some point even though people are still raising their hands you have to stop, because you've been given an hour. How do you get it gracefully stopped? Look at your watch, and say, "We have time for just two more questions." Or "I know we must be out of here by nine-thirty; let me take one more quick question. I'd be happy to answer any other questions after the session." What these comments do is let people know that you're under a time constraint (whether it's true or not), so the people who do not get their questions answered do not feel that you have brushed them off.

THE VITAL *SECOND* CONCLUSION

What do you do last? You pause one last time, you smile, and then you deliver your **second** conclusion with great force and enthusiasm. One of the most significant aspects of an entire presentation is the few words that you deliver at the very end of your session: your second conclusion. Most speakers do not have a second conclusion. They have a weak shrug, a soft comment such as, "Well, I guess that's it." Or, "Well, I haven't got any more." Or sometimes they're asked by someone to report that lunch is in the next room, or worse yet, that cocktails are being served in the vendor's area. What kind of an ending is that for your material? What kind of an ending is that for you?

You want to have prepared a short, punchy statement which is the true essence of your message. It may be as short as four or five words. You may simply say, "Make it happen!" Or, "Make this commitment and change your life." Or, "Send your check today, you'll never regret it." Or, "Write your congressman. We **can** have clean air." Your second conclusion is some memorable phrase or sentence that you can deliver with great emphasis—because it is short and dynamic.

What's significant about the second conclusion? First, you leave the audience with your words ringing in their ears. And I'm very serious about that. The last sound that you hear in a given period is replayed in your head over and over. You want your audience to replay your ringing challenge or strong statement. Second, as indicated, you want the session to end with your message, rather than with a limp shrug of shoulders or a housekeeping message from someone else.

Once you hear someone else deliver a strong second conclusion, once you deliver one yourself, you will be so impressed and so moved by it as a closing device that you will always have one in mind. Indeed you will always have one prepared. It is the difference between a weak, limp, trailing-off close and a triumphant finish.

POINTS TO REMEMBER

1. Take as many questions as you can (unless you are not prepared to answer any).
2. Be brief; don't give another speech.
3. Have a second conclusion to end everything.

The TO DO List:

Prior to the next meeting where you will be asked questions (whether or not you give a speech), jot down a list of what some of those questions may be.

CHAPTER SEVENTEEN

RESPONDING TO QUESTIONS— THINKING ON YOUR FEET

After your careful priming of the audience, a hand goes up. How should you respond to the question? Answer the question briefly so that you can respond to as many questions as possible during the time allotted without, of course, making your answers so terse that they seem rude or abrupt. Here are some general guidelines to support your understanding about the purpose of the question and answer period. (The material in this chapter is condensed and updated from my book *THINKING ON YOUR FEET Answering Questions Well, Whether You Know The Answer—Or NOT!*)

HOW CAN YOU BE SUCCESSFUL?

- Listen
- Pause to organize
- Repeat the question
- Provide main support; clue for follow-up
- Stop.

First, it is important to listen very carefully. Your adrenalin is pumping because your speech has gone well, and you are in a state of excitement. You may be anticipating many things and not listening as carefully as you should to the question as it is being given.

Second, pause. Take time to focus your thoughts. No one is going anywhere. Give yourself permission to prepare the best response out of the many that you could give. Nod. Move forward slightly. Think. Speak when you are ready.

Third, repeat the question as part of your answer. There are many reasons to repeat. Not everyone in the audience will have heard the question so include them by letting them know what the question was. Repeating the question also buys extra time to organize your thoughts; what you say will be the appropriate response, rather than just the answer that first comes to your mind. Yet another reason to repeat the question is that the answer to the question is only half of the information. The question plus the answer forms the whole fact, opinion, or observation. Half of it is not very helpful and not at all forceful or dynamic. There are some questions you may not wish to answer at all fully, yet if you give only the answer, your response seems too terse and curt. When you repeat the question as a part of your answer, you're able to make the response sound long enough, even though the answer itself is brief.

There are two basic ways that you can repeat the question. One is as a question, and the other is as part of your answer. If the question is, "How long have you been a professional speaker?" response number one is: "How long have I been a professional speaker? Twenty years, counting tonight." Or, "I have been a professional speaker for over twenty years."

Fourth, provide support and a clue for a follow-up question. Remember that the goal is brief answers to provide time for many questions. Provide first the major reason, primary explanation, or most significant factor. For example, "What do you like about public speaking?" "What I like best about public speaking is that it gives me the opportunity to help other people become more knowledgeable."

If, in the interest of being complete, you would like to give more than one piece of support, you can phrase your response in such a way that you encourage a follow-up. Provide a clue: "There are many aspects of public speaking that I like. The most satisfying one is that it gives me. . . ." The perceptive seeker (or someone else) is encouraged to ask, "What are some of the others?" Other clues work this way: "There are several reasons to practice before giving a speech. The most important one is. . . ."

If the response to the question needs more depth for this particular audience, number or enumerate in the same way you number oral guidelines, to help your audience follow the parts to the answer. "Three aspects of public speaking make it especially satisfying. First, it gives me the opportunity to . . . second, . . . and third. . . ." Or, "There are three reasons you should practice before a speech: first . . . second . . . third. . . ."

Finally, stop—without giving another speech. Take the next question.

RESPONDING WELL TO DIFFICULT QUESTIONS

The next question comes and it's a question which is long, confused, or vague in some way. If you try to answer the question as it is asked, your answer is also apt to be long, confused, or vague. The strategy is to get a better question. You can do that in several ways: You may ask the person to repeat the question; you may ask a question of your own; you may ask the questioner to define a term or concept that she has used; or, you may define or clarify some aspect yourself as a part of your answer. All four of these strategies will help you to come closer to giving the information that the questioner was truly seeking. The strategies usually turn the question into one that is easy to answer, because it is clearer. These strategies also buy you a little extra time to compose your thoughts.

Remember that the first thought that comes to your mind is often not the best response, especially to a difficult question. Buying a few seconds of time will help you to sort through the many things you might say to respond with the words that are most appropriate for this particular audience in this particular situation.

When getting a better question to answer, remember that your goal is to communicate with people, and if you answer something which is not what the questioner was looking for, you not only confuse him, you may also confuse other people in the audience. You do not have to answer every question just the way it's asked. You are the authority, the person at the front of the room. Take the opportunity to modify a question slightly as you repeat it or to adjust your response if it seems important to do so. Imagine that the question is "Why do speakers charge such high fees?" As a seasoned speaker you might modify that question slightly as you repeat it as part of your answer: "Speakers base their fees on their expertise. It takes years to become an expert."

Too many people feel that they must answer every question exactly the way it's asked. Such responders get in trouble, by bringing up information they're not certain of, or by bringing up entirely new topics. When you are responding to questions from an audience or questions which the media is asking, you keep in the front of your mind that many people in addition to the individual who asked the question are going to be hearing your answer. It is possible to answer the question to the satisfaction of the person who asked it, but at the same time confusing or irritating the much larger audience who is also going to hear or read your response. In this context it is wise to remember the expression, "the greatest good for the greatest number." One of my favorite responses came from Carol Burnett. At the beginning of her show, as some of you remember, she came in front of the curtain to take questions from the audience. One night, a voice came out of the audience, "Do you remember your most embarrassing moment?" Carol smiled and responded, "Yes." And after a tiny pause, "Next question?"

HEDGE PROFESSIONALLY

Before mass communication, a person could answer a question one way in one town and a slightly different way in another town without creating a problem. Now, with instant satellite communications, the answer is the answer; if you recognize that a more generic answer is sometimes appropriate, then you will employ a strategy called "hedging." Hedging has a bad reputation; however, it is appropriate to hedge and even necessary to hedge sometimes. You can be successful hedging so long as you remain in control and have a very professional delivery of your response.

One method for hedging is to speak to one aspect of the question that is asked. A question typically has many different facets or parts, and the main facet may be something which you are not prepared to respond to, or which it is not appropriate to respond to at this time. You hedge by speaking with authority and credibility about another aspect of the question. You will often satisfy the listener, especially if he was simply looking for more information. If you do not satisfy the listener, he (or someone else in the audience) may ask a follow-up question. In any event, you will have had a longer time to think about the topic; your response when the question is re-asked will likely be better than it would have been the first time.

A second hedging strategy that is extremely successful is refocusing the question by building a bridge. You can make your questioner feel comfortable about his own opinions and about you; you can also help to move forward your own agenda. In building a bridge you first acknowledge the opinion or the observation of the seeker, and then bridge over to your own opinion or knowledge. Assume that the question is, "I don't know why we are trying to cut down our armaments when we know the Russians are still our enemy. I'm concerned about that cut." If you are a politician, your response might be, "I'm concerned about that cut too, but I'm even more concerned about the larger concept of world peace. We must do everything we can to further world peace by. . . ."

What you will have done if you are that politician is reassure the person that she has a right to her concern—

and in this case—that you share her concern, then bridging over to your agenda, an even greater concern. Examples: "I share your opinion about that, but I have an equally strong opinion about . . ." or "That concerns me too; however, I'm even more concerned about . . ."

In other situations you may not even need to agree with the concern, but you must acknowledge it: "I can understand why you might feel that way. Let me suggest to you that it is also important to consider . . ." or, "Many people feel that way, and it's a strong and valid feeling. My feeling is. . . ." If, for example, you are making a proposal on a product or service and the question is, "Your price seems very high to me. We have a great concern in our firm for keeping prices down." Your response might be, "Of course fees are important, but even more important is the quality that you will be receiving when you. . . ." Whether you agree with the concern or comment, or merely validate the person's right to have that concern or feeling, you then build the bridge over to the concern that you have.

The third possibility for hedging professionally, "discussing" the question, is useful when people use the question format instead of simply asking for more information, which is what they really want. Sometimes people do not have enough information to even ask a question appropriately—they ask one anyway, of course, because that's the accepted format in the Q & A session. A discussion of the question will satisfy the seeker and also help you sound credible and poised.

RE-DIRECT THE QUESTION

In still other situations the question is addressed to you as the speaker when you are not the best person to answer it. There are four specific approaches you might use to re-direct the question to a more appropriate person. Two require great care. First, you might turn the question back to the audience. You might say, "That question has such great bearing on our topic tonight that I would be interested in knowing how all of you in the audience feel," or, "Let's see if we can get a consensus about that question," and you ask the question to the audience. Nearly always there is someone in the audience who would like to respond, someone who has a strong opinion. That opinion usually leads to a second opinion, and sometimes a third opinion, depending how long you wish to let the audience participate. At the end of the opinions from the audience, you may add your own, or you may repeat what someone else has said: "I agree with this gentleman, who indicated . . ." or you may simply go on to the next question.

A second possibility, and this one is especially valid if you are doing a team presentation or if other members of your firm or organization are present in the audience, is to re-direct the question to a colleague. However, there are very specific rules that you must follow if you are re-directing a question to a colleague. The rules are these:

1) State the name of the person you are re-directing the question to;
2) Describe the credentials of that person;
3) Name or identify the seeker if you can;
4) Repeat the question.

These rules are important. The only person who was listening to the question was you. If you simply dump it on your colleague by saying, "Oh, that's a great question. We've got someone here who can answer that. Judy?" Judy will bust your head after the session; she hadn't been following the discussion that closely, and she did not hear the question. So you must first get her attention by using her name. You then describe her credentials, for two reasons: you're buying her a little extra time to prepare her response, and you are explaining indirectly why you are not the one answering it. She's the authority; she just got back from a conference; she recently wrote a book on that subject; she handles that part of the process. Next, you identify the seeker (either by name or gesture), if you can, so that she can begin the response to her question to that individual. And, of course, you repeat the question so that she knows the question she is to answer.

If the question is a difficult one, put the repeat of the question earlier in your comments. A re-direct might go something like this: "The question asked is how long will the production of these graphics take?" Your response: "John Smith is head of our production department. He can give you a more exact time line on how long it will take to produce these graphics for the American Widget Corporation. John?" In that case, you have worked the question into the re-direct. Another example: You work for an agricultural-chemical company. The question from the audience may be, "I'd like to use this product on my yard, but I don't know if it's safe. What can you tell me about its safety?" Your response: "Nancy Jones, our chemical engineer, can tell you about the features of this product. Nancy just returned, in fact, from a regional conference on yard care and she'll be able to give you the information that you are looking for. Nancy, would you respond to this individual's question about the safety of Product X."

Naturally, if you have done a team presentation, or if other people in the audience are members of your firm or your group, you should have talked ahead of time about the fact that you may want to re-direct questions. You will have assured them that you are going to re-direct questions following these rules, so that they will be able to respond well. In some situations, the person you are re-directing the question to may not answer it any better than you can, except that you are buying extra time so that his response will be better than if you had tried to answer it.

Another possibility for getting someone else to respond is another member of the audience. Sometimes there is someone who is truly an expert on the topic of the question being asked. If you know that person well enough to know that he likes to be called upon, likes to demonstrate his knowledge, then you may occasionally re-direct a question to that person—following these same careful re-direct rules. Sometimes it is possible to catch the eye of that expert as the question is being asked or as you repeat it; you may see an eagerness or willingness to be called upon. However, if you are any in doubt, even 1%, if the person would be interested in responding to a question, do not re-direct it. When in doubt, don't.

Finally, there is the problem of what to do about the person who has his own agenda, some little speech that he would like to make, or a complaint to express. You see that person's hand raised and you wonder what you should do. Some speaking authorities suggest that you should never let a member of the audience have the floor. There are many times when that is excellent advice, particularly in public situations where the audience is largely strangers. But in situations where that person can do you some damage if you do not call on him, then you are better off to call on him and control him than to ignore him.

Examples of such potentially damaging situations might be within your firm, within your professional organization, or any group in which that person will have a following or an audience during the break or after the meeting. What I mean by that person hurting you is his being able to get some attention on himself by saying, "Oh, she never lets anybody ask questions except the people that she likes." Or, "I never get to say anything." Those people can hurt you out in the hall when you're not around to be in control. My suggestion is this: Let that person have his say, briefly. Do not try to respond or rebut the question or comment. This is the method to use: Look directly at the person who has his hand raised, or, if the question has already been asked and you sense it is one of those situations, say something like, "Though our time is short, we would appreciate hearing your opinion about that." Then remove your eye contact from that person and do not, under any circumstances, ever look at him again. He will begin his little speech, but without your eye contact he will not speak very long in most situations. The minute his mouth closes or the minute he draws breath, say firmly, again without looking in that direction, "Thank you very much. Next question."

Risky strategy? Perhaps. But if you have people in your audience with these kinds of hidden agendas, or little speeches that they'd like to give, you are better off to learn this strategy. Learn to control the situation, and let that person have his say, so that he will have nothing to complain about after he leaves the meeting. Again, let me stress, do not try to rebut or respond to the question. You know it isn't usually a question anyway. It's usually a comment or a complaint or a gripe. Let it be said, say thank you, move on, and do not give that person eye contact again.

NON-VERBAL COMMUNICATION DURING THE Q & A SESSION

It is appropriate to be a little more relaxed in the question and answer period. If you have been speaking behind a podium, you might hold the microphone and walk out in front of the crowd. If you've been standing fairly still, try walking around a bit more. Stand with one hand in your pocket while you are waiting for questions. Even women can use this stance if their skirt has a pocket.

When you call upon a person, gesture toward them, palm up, and say, "Yes?" or "May I have your question?" or "Your question?" Give that person direct eye contact all the time that she is asking her question. Then as you are repeating the question, turn to look at the rest of the audience: "The question is . . . ," and give your response. Resist the temptation, in most cases, to look back at the seeker and say, "I hope that's what you wanted to know," or "Does that answer your question," or "I hope that's the information you had in mind." While there are some situations where it is crucial that you do that (if you are a subordinate responding to a member of the board, for example), in public situations you are simply inviting that person to ask another question. Remember that your goal is to get as many people to participate as possible. If you end the answer with eye contact for the seeker, you are encouraging a follow-up question. If you want a follow-up question, do, by all means, look back at that seeker as you finish the answer. If you do not want a follow-up question, do not regain eye contact with the person.

As a general rule, do not use someone's name unless you can use everyone's name. The people whose names you do not know feel slighted; you seem to imply that they are less important because you do not know their names. A second taboo is to begin your response with "Good question." You cannot say that for every question, and people whose questions do not get labeled as a "good question" can feel slighted or less important. If a question is truly the crux of the entire topic, and if you can respond to it with such dynamic delivery that everyone understands this importance, it may be all right to indicate that. For example, you can say, "Your question is truly the heart of this entire problem. Let me respond by saying. . . ." Provided that your delivery and your words about the question indicate its tremendous significance, people in the audience will understand that and appreciate it. Otherwise, avoid labeling questions "That's a good question," or "That's an interesting question." Simply pause, repeat the question, give your brief answer, and stop.

If it is getting late or you are calling on people that you know tend to be long-winded, it is helpful to build in a time frame: "I can take one more question if it is brief," or "Yes, you may ask a follow-up question if you will be particularly concise," or "We have just a very few minutes left. Please be brief." When you remind people that they are under a time constraint, they are much more likely to be brief than if you do not.

In an in-house or professional situation where you know people, it is generally a good idea to take questions from the senior people in the room last. You encourage the junior members of the staff or organization to feel comfortable asking their questions. After a senior person has asked his question or made his comment, typically other people are moved to silence because they feel less significant or worry that their question is less relevant or less well phrased.

POINTS TO REMEMBER

1. Answer as many questions as possible, as briefly as you can.
2. Pause until you are ready to respond.
3. Repeat the question every time.
4. Recognize that people ask questions for reasons other than just to get the specific information that the question seems to be seeking. Do not be panicked into thinking that all questions are meant to challenge you.
5. Rephrase, refocus, or re-direct questions so they are more appropriate to the audience or easier to respond to.
6. Remain in control.

The TO DO List:

Practice responses to those questions from The TO DO List after Chapter Sixteen. Brainstorm with colleagues; the differences in what people consider appropriate may surprise all of you, but you'll all profit from the exchange.

A FINAL NOTE

Immediately after any talk or presentation, debrief yourself. Evaluate the material, the visuals, the delivery, and your results. Celebrate the wonderful aspects. Resolve to work on aspects that did not shine.

Remember, becoming an outstanding speaker is a life-long process. Confidently continue the process. You CAN master *speaking to a group*!

ADDITIONAL RESOURCES

Braude, Jacob M. *Braude's Treasury of Wit and Humor*. New Jersey: Prentice-Hall, Inc., 1964.

Cogan, Elaine and Ben Padrow. *You Can Talk to (Almost) Anyone about (Almost) Anything*. Portland, Oregon: Continuing Education Publications, Portland State University, 1984.

Cooper, Dr. Morton. *Change Your Voice Change Your Life*. New York: Perennial Library, Harper & Row, Publishers, 1985.

Glass, Lillian, Ph.D. *Talk to Win — Six Steps for a Successful Vocal Image*. New York: Perigee Books, Putnam Publishing Group, 1987.

Hazel, Harry. *The Art of Talking to Yourself and Others*. Missouri: Sheed & Ward, 1987.

Humes, James C. *Roles Speakers Play*. New York: Harper & Row, Publishers, 1976.

Iapoce, Michael. *"A Funny Thing Happened on the Way to the Boardroom" — Using Humor in Business Speaking*. New York: John Wiley, 1988.

Kemp, Jerrold E. *Planning and Producing Audiovisual Materials*, Third Edition. New York: Thomas Y. Crowell, 1975.

Keogh, James E. *Power Graphics Presentations Using Your Computer*. New York: Macmillan Company, 1985.

Le Roux, Paul. *Selling to a Group*. New York: Harper & Row, Publishers, Barnes & Noble Books, 1984.

Prague, Cary N. and James E. Hammitt. *Getting Great Graphics*. Pennsylvania: TAB Books, 1985.

Sarnoff, Dorothy. *Never Be Nervous Again*. New York: Crown Publishers, Inc., 1987.

Shone, Ronald. *Creative Visualization*. New York: Thorsons Publications, Inc., 1984.

Van Ekeren, Glenn. *The Speaker's Sourcebook. Quotes, Stories and Anecdotes for Every Occasion*. New Jersey: Prentice-Hall, Inc., 1988.

Walters, Dottie, Ed. *Sharing Ideas, A Magazine for Speakers, Meeting Planners, Bureaus & Agents & Consultants*. Glendora, California: Royal Publishing, 91740.

Woodall, Marian K. *Thinking on Your Feet — Answering Questions Well, Whether You Know the Answer — or NOT!* Lake Oswego, Oregon: Professional Business Communications, 1987.

INDEX

Q

Questions & answers, 39, 45, 55-57, 91, 92, 95, 128, 159, 185-190, 193-206

R

Relaxation, 96, 135, 142, 151, 152, 179, 180, 181, 182
see also nerves/nervousness
Rooms
arrangement of, 93, 119-122, 132, 165, 182
preparing, 36, 117-119
size of, 31, 118-119, 123, 147
visualizing, 30, 119

S

Sales/selling, 26, 29, 37, 43, 49, 89, 91-101, 115, 142, 191, 199-202
Second conclusion, 173, 190-192
Slides, see visuals
Speech
preparation of, 35, 37, 40-43, 44, 50-51, 73-75, 85-87, 129
delivery of, 27, 134-137, 147, 151-152, 161, 163, 165 173-176, 179, 183-184, 204
see also delivery
types of, 26-28, 31, 42-44, 46, 47-49, 68, 81-82
see also extemporaneous
see also manuscript
goals of, 26-29, 34
Stand/standing, 27-28, 31, 54, 93, 120, 144, 145, 149, 165, 169, 182, 204
Structure, 33, 35, 47-49, 73-75, 77, 78, 80, 85, 93, 98, 173
see also oral guidelines

T

Team presentation(s), 36, 89-101, 131, 137, 200, 201
see also panel discussions
Thesis sentence, 44, 51, 55, 73, 74, 77-79, 81, 86, 159, 173
Tone, 87, 153, 154, 157
Tool kit, 132, 164
Training, 27, 43, 63, 64, 65, 66, 67, 68, 70, 71, 79, 84

V

Videotape, 126, 136, 165, 175
Visualization, 30, 57, 135-136, 146
Visuals
types of, 53, 105-115, 164, 167, 168-169
preparation of, 103-105
using, 115, 123, 125, 126, 163-167, 168-171, 175
Voice
as speech instrument, 84, 85, 87, 96, 117, 124, 133-134, 153-156, 158-161, 174, 183
projection of, 27, 31, 118, 123-125, 161
see also emphasis, vocal/emphasize
see also exercises for voice
see also vocal color
Vocal color, 128, 155, 157-160

W

Warm-ups, pre-speech, 135-137, 160
Winging it, 95, 173

Marian K. Woodall, the author of *Thinking On Your Feet* and *Speaking To A Group*, is available to speak or to present seminars on these topics and a wide range of other oral communications topics. Her professionalism, enthusiasm, and lively style will highlight your meeting or conference.

Additional copies of the book *Speaking To A Group* are available for $15.95. Copies of the book *Thinking On Your Feet* are available for $9.95. A two-cassette audio tape package (almost two hours total listening time) is also available at $19.95. Please add shipping charge of $1.55 to the total cost of your order. VISA and MasterCard welcome.

Call: 800/447-5911 for orders.
      503/293-1163 for inquiries.

PBC
PROFESSIONAL BUSINESS COMMUNICATIONS
11830 S.W. Kerr Parkway, Suite 350
Lake Oswego, Oregon 97035

Please send copies of *THINKING ON YOUR FEET*

_____ book @ \$9.95   _____ audio tape package @ \$19.95

Please send _____ copies of *SPEAKING TO A GROUP* @ \$15.95

■ add \$1.55 shipping to the total amount of the order ■

_____
Name

_____
Address

_____
City   /   State   /   Zip Code

Please send copies of *THINKING ON YOUR FEET*

_____ book @ \$9.95   _____ audio tape package @ \$19.95

Please send _____ copies of *SPEAKING TO A GROUP* @ \$15.95

■ add \$1.55 shipping to the total amount of the order ■

_____
Name

_____
Address

_____
City   /   State   /   Zip Code

Please send copies of *THINKING ON YOUR FEET*

_____ book @ \$9.95   _____ audio tape package @ \$19.95

Please send _____ copies of *SPEAKING TO A GROUP* @ \$15.95

■ add \$1.55 shipping to the total amount of the order ■

_____
Name

_____
Address

_____
City   /   State   /   Zip Code

NOTES

COLOPHON

Speaking To A Group is first published in January, 1990.

Book typography and design by Jeff Levin of Pendragon Graphics in Beaverton, Oregon, on a Compugraphic MCS 10/8400. The text typeface is CG Melliza, which is a design derived from Hermann Zapf's Melior. The headings are set in Microstyle Bold.

Cover design and illustrations by Debra Lindland.

Author photograph by Joseph Photographer.

Printed by McNaughton & Gunn, Inc. of Ann Arbor, Michigan, on 55 pound Natural, an acid-free paper.